Can the Black Church Save Young Black America?

Closing the Educational Achievement Gap

Can the Black Church Save Young Black America?

Closing the Educational Achievement Gap

Dr. Temeca L. Richardson

Cover Design by Lynnise N. Davis

Much Lov 2 Give, LLC

This book is intended for a general audience, does not purport to give legal advice and is not intended as a substitute for professional assistance and therefore no individual should undertake the recommendations contained herein without careful study and critical consideration. The author and publisher make no warranties or representation as to the effectiveness of the suggestions contained herein for specific readers and their specific situations. Because no two situations may be the same, and it is recommended to always consult with professionals. The publisher and author disclaim any responsibility for adverse affects resulting directly or indirectly from information contained herein.

For further information, please contact:
Temeca L. Richardson, Ed.D.
6616 Pallazzo Way, Elk Grove, CA 95757
e-mail at: book@muchlov2give.org
website: www.muchlov2give.org

Book design by:
Arbor Books Inc.
19 Spear Road, Suite 301
Ramsey, NJ 07446
www.arborbooks.com

Printed in the United States of America

Can the Black Church Save Young Black America?
Dr. Temeca L. Richardson

1. Title 2. Author 3. Instruction

Library of Congress Control Number: 2006908144

ISBN-10: 0-9789560-0-1
ISBN-13: 978-0-9789560-0-4

ACKNOWLEDGEMENTS

"…with God, ALL things are possible." Matt. 19:26. It has only been with him and through him that I have had the courage, the discipline, and the faith to complete this book. To God be the glory! To my Sorors of the greatest sorority on the planet, Delta Sigma Theta, Sorority Inc., you continue to inspire me to do and be all that I can be. Specifically, (and in no particular order) Madam President, C. Lynn Carrier, Linda "L.B." Brown, Belva Flowe, Niema Winchester, Lynnise "my lil sis" Davis, Felicia Billoups, Shannon "BBS and Number" Coleman, Kimberly Clinton, Myisha "Wesh" Johnson, Frances "Frannie Mae" Johnson, Courtney D. Havener, Debora Jett, Ahmanal Dorsey, Erica King-Waring, Audia Wells, Sandi Patterson, June "the Bishop-Attorney" Powells-Mays, Latrece Smothers, Linda White, and the "Delta Dears." To my family, Pastor and Prophetess Hightower and Family, Brother and Sister Early and Family, my adopted family Pastor and First Lady Buckhalter and Family, Mr. and Mrs. Wilson and Family, Pastor (my daddy) and First Lady Richardson and Family, the Watts and family, the Alvidrezes, and the Boatman-Pattersons.

TABLE OF CONTENTS

INTRODUCTION

The Three–Part System to Rear a Child:
the Family, the School, the Church

The Family Unit

To begin this book in the simplest form, according to Webster's dictionary, the family unit is "the primary social group; parents and children." For good or for ill, the family unit—its structure, its influence—is perhaps the single most critical aspect in the shaping of the young mind. Regardless of culture or creed, the family unit forms the basis of our learning and our emotional support (or the lack thereof), and shapes our overall mental and physical development.

On a primary level, parents are responsible for even the most basic aspects of a child's growth. Motor skills such as walking, speech development and the identification of dangerous objects are directly swayed by the parental figure. These skills may seem rather rudimentary, something that can be learned without much teaching, but they play a fundamental role in the creation of a child's subconscious, psyche and eventual learning capacity. As such, all parents, especially parents of color, should make it a point to more consistently focus on the cultivation of these skills during a child's beginning years (from birth to age five).

As a child reaches the age that requires him/her to head off to school, the role of the parent in his/her life amplifies. However, when the data is studied closely, (as this book aims to do), a bleak picture emerges—one that features a rather sizable contingent of parents who finds the task of developing a proper student a bit too daunting. Raising a driven child is a tremendous amount of work and a rather trying responsibility, to be certain. But make no mistake: the duty is not without its rewards.

Unfortunately, if we center on the topic of children of color in particular, parents today seem all too willing to blindly leave the task of instilling academic skills and behavioral conduct solely in the hands of the schools. The crux of this book is that we, as families of color, are not attentive enough to the educational needs of our children. And the alarming result of this lack of involvement is the already staggering (and widening) academic achievement gap between children of color and their White and Asian classmates.

Is it possible that, when compared to the direct academic involvement displayed by White and Asian parents, Black and Hispanic caregivers are not taking an active enough roll in school activities? Is it possible that there is not enough awareness, as a whole, of a child's extracurricular interests? On a large scale, the data suggests that parents of color do not attend teacher conferences. In addition, there is very little minority opinion voiced at important school gatherings such as School Site Council or PTA meetings.

There is perhaps a valid explanation for this. Parents of color simply are unaccustomed to the need for participating in such measures. In the past, PTA meetings were not as necessary because the society of color tended to be so much more communal. Historically, people of color have worked together within their own communities in the unified hope of achieving a common goal.

Because of the complacency that seems to be bred by today's society, our negligence toward our own most valuable and historical resources, our strange and damaging fixation on opportunistic capitalism and our inability to keep the church involved in the education of our children, as a unit, have led us away from many shared goals that could potentially propel our entire culture forward. As Black and Brown parents and church leaders, we must find a way to refocus our communal priorities back to our children before it's too late.

As Black and Brown parents and church leaders, we must find a way to refocus our communal priorities back to our children before it's too late.

Turning attention to the school system, this chapter suggests that specific data collected from a large cross-section of American high schools has presented a rather bleak outlook beginning to emerge. For example, the 2002 Public Agenda Survey noted that two of the most significant factors weighing on the gross underperformance of America's minority youth include a lack of community and inordinately low parental involvement. When compared to the numbers demonstrated by White parents, the data looks even more ominous. In summary, Black and Hispanic parents simply are not as involved with the educational advancement of their children. In 1999, only 53.8% of Black parents attended a class event (such as a choir recital or school play) and a mere 26.2% of those same parents surveyed volunteered at their child's school. For Hispanic parents, the numbers were even less encouraging. Fifty-one and a half percent suggested that they had attended a class event and only 24.5% had volunteered at their child's school. For White parents, the answers were spiked significantly towards the positive. Seventy-one point six percent claimed to have attended a class event and 42.7% volunteered at their child's school.

In 2003, the numbers continued along a similar line. Sixty-three point three percent of Black parents and 60.9% of Hispanic parents attended a class event. Only 32% of Black parents and 27.7% of Hispanic parents volunteered at their child's school, compared to 48.4% of White parents.

> We must allow the church, as the epicenter of Black and Brown society, to assume the most significant role in 'righting the ship.'

Do these statistics depict a sad crisis of educational detachment in the community of color or an alarming decline in parental interest that seems destined to endanger an entire generation of minority youth?

5

As people of color, even if we are parents who volunteer at our child's school and regularly attend PTA meetings (and there still *are* a great many of these noble parents out there), we cannot be afraid to take an honest look at our role in this crisis. We have to face the fact that a continued lack of direct involvement will impair the growth of our children and their education well into the future.

Fortunately, there is aid available. And, as this book works to suggest, that aid can and should come from the religious element of every neighborhood. In order for the church to accurately assist us as parents of color, however, we must first avoid excuse-making and finger-pointing. If we hope to shed light on and eventually fix the problem, we must heed the old and seemingly forgotten adage that it takes a village to raise a child. In other words, we must allow the church, as the epicenter of Black and Brown society, to assume the most significant role in "righting the ship."

The Task Facing America's Schools

Quite obviously, the school remains the main catalyst in educating our youth. In modern America, education is a divine right; one that ideally should ignore a child's color, socioeconomic status, primary language, home life, or educational [dis]abilities. Obviously, this is a rather utopian view. Let it be stated that at no point in this book will you find the claim that the various socioeconomic negatives assaulting our community play a part in this startling decline. Each influence has a role to play in a child's life. In order to overcome some of the more troubling influences, we must work to boost the positive ones and, ideally, gain a better sense of control over the upbringing of our children.

Six decades ago, America enjoyed a position at the world's statistical peak in subjects such as math, science and reading. Today, when compared to all other developed countries, we lag far behind in those same three disciplines. If all children, minority and low income children included, are stalling in the current educational system, then the whole country faces grave danger. Some would point to the fact that suburban and high-income children are actually doing better these days than they were in the 50s. To that, it should be suggested that we cannot examine one piece of the pie without looking at the pie in its totality.

According to the article, "How to Fix America's Schools" (*BusinessWeek*, March 19, 2001), less than half of America's children read proficiently at their grade level. U.S. 12th graders still score well below teenagers in almost every other developed country on mathematics and science tests. The 74% of students who have completed high school by the age of 18 rank the U.S. at 17th in graduation rates after decades of leading the world.

Low-income and minority students fare the worst. For example, only 29% of all fourth graders in this category read at grade level; but among low-income kids (a category that encompasses a great number of Black and Hispanic children), the figure is 13%.

As Chapter 2 will demonstrate, the achievement gap between White children and children of color, too, is growing tremendously and has become a very serious issue. Diplomatic measures such as President George W. Bush's No Child Left Behind simply do not offer the kind of initiative necessary to bridge that gap, either. While annual state-mandated tests certainly represent a step in the right direction, holding the schools more accountable for testing, on its own, is not nearly enough.

The Critical Role of the Church

There has been, is, and will always be a great need for the church to take an active role in the lives of America's Black and Brown youth. If for no other reason, religious involvement statistically demonstrates beneficial support for the mental, spiritual and emotional health of the people, especially people of color. As stated in the June 1995 publication of the *Social Science & Medicine Journal*, religion is an especially valuable mental health resource for racial minorities in the United States. The data revealed in this survey was gathered from a large community sample centering in the southeastern region of the United States. Findings include the following:

1. Frequency of church attendance is not associated with depressive symptoms among Whites, but it is among Blacks.
2. Absence of denominational affiliation triggers depressive symptoms among Blacks, but not among Whites.
3. Prayer alleviates depressive symptoms among both racial groups.

This data overwhelmingly suggests that a church presence is beneficial to almost all facets of mental and emotional development, particularly in the community of color.

A positive mental, spiritual, and emotional well being enables us to sustain a healthy lifestyle which heightens our chances of success in all aspects of our lives. In order to cultivate a healthy mentality, our children need this same constant, positive reinforcement from the church.

To take this notion a step forward and examine the *conscious* effect religion has on minority youth, the National Study of Youth and Religion offers a sample taken from religious and semi-religious American teens. Black Protestant and conservative Hispanic Protestant teens are considerably more likely than mainline White Protestant teens to say that religious faith is very or extremely important in shaping their daily lives. 69% of Black Protestant teens, 64% of conservative Black Protestant teens, and 76% of Black Baptist teens affirm that their religious faith is very or extremely important in shaping their priorities in general. These figures are relatively higher than the 43% of White Mainstream Protestant teens who state the same.

The Goal of This Book

Primarily, this book aims to take a critical look at the role that the church is or is not playing in the educational needs of Black and Brown communities. At its core, these pages represent a call to Black, Hispanic and inner-city churches to take a greater sense of responsibility for the education of the children of color within their own congregations. The church must re-establish itself as a force in the educational future of Black and Brown America.

> The church must re-establish itself as a force in the educational future of Black and Brown America.

This book is divided into four main sections. Section One highlights many of the problems that plague children of color. Among these tribulations are: assessment of self, the perspective on a personal role in society and, to some degree, the shortage of highly qualified teachers (particularly teachers of color) in schools with a high concentration of minorities. In addition, this section scrutinizes many of the harsh predicaments that our children face in the Black and Brown community, centering on the question of why the achievement gap is continuing to widen year after year.

The next section focuses on the historical perspective of the Black church and its involvement in every major Civil Rights movement in our nation's history. This section also illustrates the startling disparities between the Mormon church's distinct, effective approach in preparing their youth for advancement in the modern world versus the Black church's disjointed and, in some cases, relative non-approach.

The third section offers demonstrable solutions for what the church of color could do to rectify young Black and Brown America's failing educational standards. This segment will pinpoint the drastic results in education that will occur if this impediment isn't addressed. It also takes a look at other organizations that have historically proven to be qualified support systems for children. Perhaps their track record of success will aid the church in developing programs designed to close the substantial achievement gap. This information is then synergized into a roadmap of sorts that will help the Black and Brown church to navigate toward such an end.

The final section examines the degree of social and educational destruction that can and will occur if changes are not made. If the church does not get involved on a large scale, already alarming statistics in areas such as teenage pregnancy, drug use and gang participation will continue to rise. The number of jobs will decrease for minimally skilled and lesser-educated workers. The future of the church for our youth will likewise be devastated.

In the end, this book represents a call to action. One should not simply agree with its content and then leave the work to someone else. Each individual must take strides to improve matters for our children. Regardless of personal power within the church, it is the responsibility of *everyone* to do his/her part.

PART ONE

The Problem

Train up a child in the way he should go,
and when he is old, he will not depart from it.
—Proverbs 22:6
King James Version

CHAPTER 1

Identification of Self:
Shaping the Mind of the Minority Child

One of the greatest debates in modern theory is that of nature versus nurture. According to the natural theory of human evolution, humans are genetically predisposed to take on their various mental, physical and even social qualities. Theorists that support the nurture end of the debate suggest that it is our environment and our personal experiences that shape our present and changing identity.

Given these equally valid representations of personal development, we can decide to argue, as several theorists have, that Blacks and Hispanics are genetically inferior or genetically predisposed to be less intelligent than their White counterparts. It seems, however, that this perspective is shaped by vast amounts of subjectivity. As suggested by the extraordinarily controversial *The Bell Curve: Intelligence and Class Structure in American Life* by Richard Hurrnstein and Charles Murray (1994), genetic predisposition is the main reason why children of color fair worse educationally than White children.

In order to contradict such a seemingly narrow-sighted opinion, we must first investigate several aspects of the environment (nurture) that aid in the development of self for children of color.

Minority Images Depicted by the Media

If we are to discuss the media in any kind of general sense, then it would be prudent to analyze local newscasts, entertainment television, and a sampling of advertising campaigns. Black and Brown people in America are constantly bombarded with commercials and media influences that can be summarized as negative. Take, for instance, paid programs that allow you to get rich quick for a low, low introductory price instead of learning financial discipline; and let us not forget the highly romanticized ideology of sports and entertainment (which tend to project images of the poor kid from the "hood" making it big, becoming a megastar, and gaining obscene riches, all before the age of 25).

The worst part about all of this is that it seems to make for good marketing, with minority earnings quickly becoming a thriving resource for the enterprising retailer. According to CN-

The most obvious capitalist grab on minority dollars was made evident when the makers of the Lincoln Navigator teamed up with hip-hop mogul Sean "P. Diddy" Combs.

NMoney.com, in 2003, the most obvious capitalist grab on minority dollars was made evident when the makers of the Lincoln Navigator teamed up with hip-hop mogul Sean "P. Diddy" Combs to make a special line of SUVs that included three DVD players, six plasma television screens, two Sony Playstations, and vibrating seats. In the summer of 2004, the makers of the Dodge Chrysler 300 teamed up with superstar rapper Snoop Doggy Dog in a national campaign that involved

Snoop and Lee Iacocca golfing and chatting about the former's "fly ride."

In the article entitled "Television Viewing and Perceptions about Race Differences in Socioeconomic Success" from the *Journal of Broadcasting & Electronic Media*, writer Rick Busselle Crandall exposes the imbalance of the statistical realities of poverty among Blacks in their "real lives" when compared to their image in news media presentations. In his 1996 study, Crandall shows that 27% of poor Americans were Black, but that Blacks made up roughly 63% of the presentation of poor people in the most prominent outlets of national news media. Crandall states that this overrepresentation has created a disproportionately strong link between race and poverty in the mind of the viewer. This negative assumption erroneously leads people of all nationalities to think, consciously and subconsciously, that Blacks *are* the poor in this country.

> For a young Black child who is left to his/her own devices, the damaging message becomes abundantly clear—being Black becomes a state of mind and a state of being that *equates to* being poor.

For a young Black child who is left to his/her own devices, the damaging message becomes abundantly clear: the child doesn't subconsciously think, "I am poor," but rather, "the way I am is the way that it is." In other words, being Black becomes a state of mind and a state of being that *equates to* being poor.

Turning to the concept of crime, in the *Journal of Research in Crime and Delinquency*, writers Ted Chiricos and Sarah Eschholz analyze local news programming from three television stations in Orlando, Florida for racial and ethnic content in relation to crime. Chiricos and Eschholz found that Hispanics are slightly overrepresented as criminals in relation to their numbers in the population. They also discovered that Blacks and especially Hispanics who appear as crime suspects do so in more threatening contexts than Whites. Blacks and Hispanics are far more likely to appear as criminal suspects than as victims or role models.

Professor Shanto Iyengar of UCLA presents other studies that display the increasingly heavy minority share of crime depiction in broadcast news programming over the past decade. These studies point to two qualitative features of news programming: violence and race. Professor Iyengar states that, "Not only does news coverage highlight violent crime, it also links the issues of race and crime by over-representing minorities in the role of violent criminals and by according them distinctive forms of coverage. In summary, the typical news story on crime consists of two scripts: crime is violent and criminals are non-White."

And the assault does not end when the program breaks, either. Advertisements on Black Entertainment Television (BET), one of the most popular networks among African

Americans, include frequent slots for alcohol products, Kool-Aid, "get out of debt" companies and HIV awareness commercials; all of which feature mostly minority actors. CNBC, the world business news channel, on the other hand, frequently airs commercials for Mercedes, Lexus, and BMW luxury cars, home loan ads, and spots for advisory firms; all of which feature mostly White actors.

In the realm of entertainment on television, there are two dominant portrayals of Blacks: comfortable and successful or unemployed and criminal. This dichotomized depiction of Black people seems to leave little room for a middle-ground. Blacks and Hispanics make up a small percentage of TV sitcom characters and minority families are practically non-existent in TV dramas. In the sitcom world, Blacks and Hispanics are displayed as comical, comfortable, and successful. In the shows, the characters face very little racism or discrimination.

Even in the absence of strong psychological depictions about minorities projected in the media, children of color begin to subconsciously define and redefine the concept of being a minority long before they are even allowed to spend long hours watching television. The act of categorizing members of the minority or majority culture, after all, has been in existence for centuries (long before television was first conceived) and has always been designed to classify and, in some ways, dehumanize different ethnic groups.

The Majority and the Minority

More than 200 years ago, it apparently seemed *necessary and purposeful* to subdivide Americans into four distinct racial categories, a practice that today remains unchanged. In the 2002 *Hoover Digest* article "The Myth of the Minority Majority," writer Stephan Therstrom fervently states that nineteenth century conceptions of race are alive and well in the official guidelines developed by the U.S. Office of Management and Budget's Directive No. 15, "Race and Ethnic Standards for Federal Statistics and Administrative Reporting." Promulgated on May 12, 1977, Directive No. 15 governs the statistical data that all federal agencies must gather. Directive No. 15 declares that the population of the United States is divided into four races: Whites, Blacks, Asians/Pacific Islanders, and American Indians/Alaskan Natives. Further complicating matters is the notion that there, then, exists only two ethnic groups: Hispanics and non-Hispanics. This doctrine requires all agencies of the federal government to compile data to assess the impact of their programs using these categories and these categories alone. Therstrom reveals that "the authors of Directive 15 were careful to say that these classifications should not be interpreted as being scientific or anthropological in nature." The trouble with the fact that there was nothing scientific about the categorization of America's people is that this rather arbitrary act has led to a direct shaping of many contemporary cultural values. This "race grouping" and majority/minority characterization has certainly played on the psyche of the minority child since its inception over two hundred years ago.

Value Conflicts in Education

The educational value system in America suggests that we go to school, take increasingly difficult courses, work to earn a solid Grade Point Average (GPA), attend a good college and graduate school, graduate, and find a well-paying job. These constructs hold true regardless of race, religion or geographical location. Despite all this, we still find large and ever-increasing minority households who share vastly different educational values. In many minority households, upon high school graduation, children are typically influenced to enter the workforce or guided towards service in one of the military branches. These social paths are seen as a replacement for the more traditional educational vein when the cost of college seems to place higher education out of reach.

Prior to the point when many minority families even begin to contemplate life after graduation for their children, we find demonstrable shortfalls in several key stages of the minority child's educational preparation. In low-income schools, where the majority of the student body tends to be children of color, teachers often face inordinately high numbers of students that do not complete and return their homework in a timely manner. This rarely holds true in more affluent schools, where the demographics lean primarily towards children from the majority group or children in higher socioeconomic subgroups. While the completion of homework may seem small in the grand scheme of educational preparation, it speaks very highly towards the necessary discipline that it takes to achieve high levels of educational success. In addition, the failure to complete homework tends to separate the child from the teacher, who often views the act as a lack of interest on the part of the student. The trouble with this factor is that it is a bit too narrow. Many times, particularly in the case of a child living in an impoverished home where he/she may be required to tend to the younger siblings or take on a night job to help the family pay the bills, homework just isn't as doable as it might be in another home. In cases such as these, a child is too often punished for circumstances that are beyond his/her control. Classes that require the completion of homework as a large percentage of the final grade are therefore unfairly bent against these otherwise bright and driven children.

Another disparity between many minority and majority households is the significance placed upon standardized test scores. Instead of focusing on their ability to score well on standardized tests, minority families tend to measure the success of their children on whether or not they are receiving As and Bs on their report cards. The trouble with this focus is that As and Bs in low-income schools do not tend to compare favorably with As and Bs in more affluent schools. Similarly put, an A in a poor community simply does not stack up to an A in a wealthy one. Sadly, many parents of color are not aware of this fact. They continue to take lettered grades at face value while simultaneously writing off the importance of standardized test scores as just another unfair government mandate. What they do not realize is that standardized test scores, because of their nationalized metrics, give a more accurate indication of how a particular child compares academically to other students in his/her age group across the nation—fairly or unfairly.

According to various 1990-2005 Reading and Mathematics Assessment statistics that were derived from the U.S. Department of Education, the National Center for Education Statistics, and the National Assessment of Educational Progress (NAEP), there continues to be a gap in achievement between White and Black students as well as White and Hispanic students. The information appears below in Table 1.

Subject, race/ethnicity, and grade	1990	1992	1994	1996	1998	2000	2002	2003	2005
White-Black and White-Hispanic gaps in average reading and mathematics scores, by grade: Various years, 1990–2005									
Reading									
White-Black gap									
Grade 4	—	32	38	—	32	34	30	31	29
Grade 8	—	30	30	—	26	—	27	28	28
White-Hispanic gap									
Grade 4	—	27	35	—	32	35	28	28	26
Grade 8	—	26	24	—	27	—	26	27	25
Mathematics									
White-Black gap									
Grade 4	32	35	—	34	—	31	—	27	26
Grade 8	33	40	—	41	—	40	—	35	34
White-Hispanic gap									
Grade 4	20	25	—	25	—	27	—	22	20
Grade 8	24	28	—	30	—	31	—	29	27

Table 1

Though the data shows that the numbers have fluctuated by no more than seven points up or down over the years, despite our best efforts, the gap quite simply *is not closing*.

According to a September 2004 article published in *Black Issues in Higher Education*, the average score of Black SAT takers dipped one point on the verbal section of the exam (to

430), compared to the 2003 average. The average math score of Blacks rose one point to 427, on the other hand. Compared to the scores of ten years prior (in 1994), the average verbal score among Black students in 2004 enjoyed a two-point gain while the average math score was up six points. Overall, however, Black students still score the lowest on the exam when compared to other minority groups. In general, most minority groups still score lower when compared to their White counterparts. See Table 2:

2004 SAT RESULTS		
STUDENTS	AVERAGE SCORES	
	Verbal	Math
American Indian	483	488
Asian	507	577
Black	430	427
Mexican American	451	458
Puerto Rican	457	452
Other Hispanic	461	465
White	528	531

Table 2

Another important and often overlooked fact to remember is that, when studies show the 2004 average scores of African American children being up only a few more points in comparison to the scores of ten years ago, it becomes increasingly clear that, when comparing African American scores with White scores, the achievement gap will take decades to close. If we may assume that the White scores remain roughly the same, if we continue to see such middling improvements to the median African American score, the achievement gap could take 50 years (assuming a two-point gain per year) or as many as 100 years (assuming a one-point gain per year) to close. Consider those figures for a moment. Can an initiative that will theoretically take anywhere from a half to a full century to come to fruition really be considered progress? Also, considering the many variables and influences placed upon the average child in modern times, how likely is it that these trends will remain on an upward slope? This question is especially startling considering the fact that Table 2 does not show an across-the-board improvement. Rather, for each success, we see at least one regression.

The Church

When looking back on many of the pressures and psychological stressors that children of color face, it becomes increasingly clear that they need a great deal of support. The important questions become quite evident: How can the church help to improve the child of color's outlook on their societal and educational role? What steps can the church take to begin raising the self-confidence and self-awareness levels of the minority child? How does the church begin to educate the child on his/her ancestral past? Should the church encourage minority parents to use racial socialization to solve some of these issues?

In hindsight, it is perhaps not an understatement to advocate that there are a number of approaches that the Black church could and perhaps should take to help shape the perception of the Black child socially, emotionally and spiritually, especially given the influences that children of color are facing in the 21st century. When the data so evidently suggests that religion plays an exceptionally important role in the shaping of everyday social values (indeed, a potentially stronger role than the census construct or even the local news can play), does the notion that an all-too-large cross-section of minority children are failing in school signify an unacceptable lack of leadership and activism on the part of the church? Before we can even begin to answer that question, we must further examine some of the troubling trends that have emerged among Black and Brown students over the course of the past three decades.

CHAPTER 2

The Crisis of Education in the
Community of Color

A distressing educational crisis has befallen the community of color. The crisis represents a significant calamity; one that is both virtually and literally killing the potential of our youth. Many great minds have come forward to place blame on one outside influence or another and we have read and heard about many driving factors that have led such a large number of minority children to fail. But whatever the predominant cause, whatever argument can be made, there seems to be one universally accepted opinion: our children are following a most discouraging path.

The survival of the community of color, as with any community, is predicated upon the success of the youth. Unfortunately, several factors continue to hinder the simple likelihood of our children's success. Among these factors are soaring high school dropout rates, abhorrently low college enrollment rates, a distinct lack of self-motivation among boys of color, abysmal fourth grade test scores, the alarming absence of minority children from the achievement classes of the average public school, the shortage of quality teachers in poverty-stricken schools, the high number of out-of-field educators teaching in impoverished schools and the overrepresentation of children of color in special education classes.

Fortunately, amidst all this adversity, akin to all these numbers and figures and well-laid philosophies, an overarching solution emerges. I posit that it is time for us, as parents and church leaders of color, to quit placing blame on outside influences and finally step in and help our educational system to put an end to this most disheartening situation. Moreover, we have to finally come to an understanding that the educational troubles of our children cannot and should not be drawn from a cry against White America. We must take a greater sense of responsibility for the state that our schools are in, for the shortage of teachers of color, for the educational disposition of our children and for the many bright futures that we, through our inactivity, have been complicit in destroying.

Make no mistake, I do not intend to suggest that communities of color are solely responsible for the socioeconomic conditions surrounding the public school system or Black and Hispanic neighborhoods. There are certainly still a great many obstacles to overcome. What I suggest, however, is that the obstacles are not insurmountable. There is so much more that we can do as a community and, most importantly, as a church.

In short, it is time for the Black church to take a stand. It is time for us to recognize our recent lack of contribution and take steps to become a part of the solution. So, in response to this call, I present the following pages, which do their part to quantify the issues that continue to plague children of color. To begin, this assessment offers a look at the conditions of the schools that our children attend.

Impoverished vs. Affluent Schools

If drawing from an example first highlighted on the Oprah Winfrey show may be allowed, an examination of the talk show host's take on the conditions of public schools in the Chicago area is certainly warranted. The inequality of education depicted was just too startling to ignore. The truly shocking aspect of the special was that America, as a viewing audience, reacted as though it were the first time that it had been exposed to the inadequacies of impoverished schools (when compared to the thriving status of the affluent schools located mere miles down the road).

The program showcased two schools: one, a low-income community high school and the other, an affluent suburban high school. It certainly could not have taken long for the average viewer to realize which school had the upper hand. Perhaps owing to the latter institution's academic success, the suburban school featured an Olympic-sized swimming pool, a gym and fitness center, state-of-the-art classrooms and educational equipment and a 'rigorous course curriculum'. In complete juxtaposition, the students from the low-income school were forced to begin their day by passing through a metal-detector. While there was a pool, it had been without water for more than a decade. In addition, though there was indeed a music class offered, the instruments supplied to the students were broken and insufficient in number (a veritable shade of what the suburban students had access to). And, finally, the grand total of advanced placement (AP) classes for the impoverished school was two.

But while the April 11 and 12, 2006 shows were deeply affecting, Oprah merely scratched the surface. These problems are not confined to the south side of Chicago. In addition to the factors listed in the introduction, community schools (particularly schools with a high enrollment of minority students) tend to have minimal resources, under-qualified teachers, overcrowded classrooms, and a higher number of children classified as having 'special needs'. All of this is a far cry from the highly-credentialed teachers at affluent schools. Rarely in an impoverished school will one find the kind of newly printed textbooks so common in the suburbs. And the sheer numbers of special education students at affluent schools are far outweighed by those (often misdiagnosed) special education students at impoverished schools.

High School Dropout Rates

But perhaps it would be beneficial to drift away from the purely subjective influences and take a look at the hard numbers. For a demonstration of just how deep the rift between these two categories of institution has grown, look no further than the soaring high school dropout rates among predominantly minority schools. According to Oprah's study, the low-income school demonstrated only a 40% graduation rate among its students. A humbling number; especially when compared to the 99% graduation rate boasted by the suburban school.

The question then becomes, why is this happening? It should come as no shock that, without the nurturing support of a healthy school environment, the child of color will grow discouraged more easily than he/she otherwise would. As discussed in Chapter One, there are several significant social and environmental roadblocks that tend to influence the life of a child of color. As all of these roadblocks pile up, the load becomes increasingly more difficult for the child to bear on his/her own. As such, without the necessary support, there is a much higher tendency for a student at a largely minority school to give up hope too soon.

> ...of the students enrolled in community colleges in California, more than 70% are Black.

In an article entitled "What Can We Do to Save Our Young Men?: (*Jet Magazine*, July 10, 2006), journalist Marti Parham reveals just how readily young Black males are failing to complete a basic high school education. The article draws upon a series of recent nationwide studies, including those recorded in Ronald B. Mincy's new book *Black Males Left Behind*, to highlight the fact that more than half of all Black males who start school never actually finish. The journalist goes on to suggest that the dropout rates work as a direct influence on the rising rates of incarceration and unemployment demonstrated by the same demographic. As such, Parham adeptly points out that, as the young Black male fails, so too does the Black community.

But what about young Black women? In an article entitled "Gender Differences in Self-Perceptions and Academic Outcome: a Study of African American High School Students" (*Journal of Youth and Adolescence*, February, 2004), Jeanne Saunders, Larry Davis, Trina Williams, and James Herbert Williams suggest that the problem isn't just confined to the young men of the community. At a 56% graduation rate among the demographic, it is easy to see that young Black females aren't faring much better than their male counterparts (at 43%).

For Hispanic students, fortunes are similar. With "Latinos' Education Gap; High School Dropout Rates Remain High" (*Business Week*, August 2, 2004), James Mehring outlines the findings of author Pia Orrenius, a Federal Reserve Bank of Dallas economist. In the article, it is revealed that Orrenius employed a significant cross-section of historical data to demonstrate that the high school dropout rate for Latino immigrants (44.2%) is extraordinarily poor when compared to the combined rates of all non-Latinos (7.4%). Why are Hispanic students dropping out of school at higher rates? Orrenius posits that, "Latinos who contend with the low quality of schooling in many inner cities become discouraged from pursuing a college education and sometimes from even finishing high school." So, as high school dropout rates among communities of color increase, so too will college enrollment rates decrease. As such, it would be prudent to examine the statistics.

College Enrollment

As is the case with any discussion on minority enrollment in America's colleges and universities, I would be remiss if I failed to discuss Affirmative Action. Its shortcomings seem to be the reactionary's first clue as to why so many minorities are failing to apply to and graduate from an institution of higher learning. As indicated in the article, "College Admissions Mixed Bag for Blacks: Debate over Affirmative Action May Affect Application Figures" (*Black Enterprise*, August, 2005), the repeal of Affirmative Action seems to have affected a decline in Black acceptance into majority-White schools. It should be pointed out, however, that this is not necessarily because the schools in question are considering fewer Black applicants. Rather, it seems that fewer Black applicants are considering majority-White schools. Aisha Jefferson, the article's author, stresses the point that, following the controversial Supreme Court decision regarding the University of Michigan's Affirmative Action policy, the school experienced a backlash in relation to the number of African American applicants and enrollees. Even though the eventual decision (in 2003) proved to be made in favor of minorities and women, Black students, by and large, still seemed to feel bruised by the commotion that the lawsuits had raised.

During the year following the decision, the number of Black freshman applicants and enrollees to the University fell by 28% and nearly 15%, respectively.

But the handling of Affirmative Action, clearly, is not the only influence to blame for the decline. Another critical factor to consider is the perception of achievement among Black students seeking a higher education. With their article, "Black Male Achievement and the Community College" (*Community College Week Magazine*, March 14, 2005), Edward C. Bush and Lawson Bush reveal that the Black male perception of higher education seems to have changed very little since the middle 1960s, when a two-year degree provided access to higher-paying jobs and lent a stronger sense of marketability in the workforce. According to the article, of the students enrolled in community colleges in California, more than 70% are Black. What's more, the review of student performance data provided by the California Chancellor's Office for Community Colleges indicates that, despite serving as the overwhelming majority, Black men are the lowest performing subgroup when it comes to the percentage of degrees earned, rates of persistence, and average cumulative grade point average among all community college students. In a 2003 study known as *Beware of False Promises*, the Bushes suggest potential reasons for this incredible discrepancy in performance. The study shows that Black men are far less likely to meet with their instructors than other subgroups and, additionally, are less likely to be involved in extracurricular activities.

Even in Historically Black Colleges and Universities (HBCUs), where one might expect a Black student to feel more comfortable with his/her peers and advisors, the retention rates among the demographic are quite low. Journalist Glenda Prime, in her article entitled "A Missing Element in the Retention Discussion" (*Black Issues in Higher Education*, December 6, 2001), reveals that, out of the thousands of Black students entering four-year colleges and universities, only 40% of them ever reach graduation. She posits that traditional evaluation methods of students need to be reexamined. While it is irrefutable that GPA contributes greatly to whether a student decides to remain enrolled in college, Prime takes things one step further, suggesting that, as a construct, the measure is unfairly weighted against minority students. She claims that African American students and other minorities (which she calls "nontraditional students") are not necessarily failing to learn (as their low GPAs might suggest), but rather, are placed at a disadvantage considering the methods traditionally employed to assess the retention

Black males are more likely to be identified as behaviorally disorded than black females or any other minority demographic for that matter.

of information. As such, these traditional methods of educational measure such as GPA and written tests should perhaps be reassessed.

Hispanic students should not be left out of the argument, either. With his article "Education Gaps among U.S. Hispanics" (*Diverse Issues in Higher Education*, March 23, 2006), David Pluviose reveals that, according to a recent report released by the National Research Council, Hispanics (especially immigrant Hispanics) remain at the bottom of the economic ladder in job acquisition, due mainly to a lack of formal schooling and English proficiency. In the article, Dr. Marta Tienda, the chair of the National Research Council panel, argues, "Hispanic children aren't being pushed towards college during their middle school years. By the time the students reach high school, many are too far behind academically to make college a realistic option. Others don't feel the need to attend college because none of their classmates are."

And so, if admissions programs fail, retention programs remain ineffective, assessment programs are biased, school-run motivational programs fall short, financial aid does little to attract interest and minority graduation rates continue to decline, who or what else is left to come to our aid? Before I attempt to answer that question, I would like to throw another intriguing complication into the mix; the academic performance level of girls of color seems to differ greatly from the performance level of boys of color. The next segment examines why.

Black/Hispanic Girls vs. Black/Hispanic Boys

In the report, "Are Boys Being Left Behind?" (*Cherokee Sentinel*, February 22, 2006), editor Dwight Otwell analyzes the findings from a January 30 Newsweek article regarding the significant discrepancy between males and females of color within the Cherokee County School District. Otwell relates that Black and Hispanic females in the district, as a whole, scored better than their male counterparts on their end-of-course exams. 83.3% of Hispanic females scored at or above a Level III (which is a passing grade). 87.5% of Black females scored similar marks. Conversely, only 44.4% of Hispanic males and 50% of Black males scored at or above a Level III. So, why the dichotomy of scoring levels? These students all grew up in the same communities and attended the same elementary schools, after all. As both Otwell and the Newsweek article that he references state, boys are twice as likely as girls to be diagnosed with learning disabilities and placed in special education classes at a young age. In support of this claim, these same Cherokee County schools, on December 1, 2005, listed 359 males as members of their disabled student population. Only 156 females qualified under the same category. This is a 70/30 split.

Returning to *Gender Differences in Self-Perceptions and Academic Outcomes*, Saunders, Davis, Williams and Williams also found that Black females are more favorably oriented toward high school completion than their male counterparts. A survey conducted of 243 Black high school sophomores (136 females and 107 males) from an urban community in the Midwest demonstrated that Black females reported significantly stronger intentions to complete the school year when compared to the intentions of Black males. These sentiments were reflected in the numbers, too, as the average GPA for females in the district was 2.20 while that of the males was a paltry 1.85.

But what reasons could Black males have for approaching the school environment so differently from females? The first reason seems to be supported by an extraordinarily uniform tendency for young Black males to have lower marks in reading and conduct. In addition, a startling number of these unfortunate students have failed one or more grade levels. Black males are also more likely to bear the harsh reprisal of corporal punishment, receive a suspension, and to be identified as behaviorally disordered than Black females (or any other minority demographic, for that matter). Obviously, it isn't long before these sorts of measures begin to affect not only school performance, but lead to social isolation and stigmatization as well. Given these trends, it should come as no surprise that the majority of the Black males included in the survey stated that they viewed school as a hostile environment, citing frustrations in their academic efforts.

The same study revealed that Black females tend to have more positive experiences in school, leading to an increase in the confidence levels associated with academic skill. They were far more likely to report receiving rewards (rather than punishments) from the school system. Overall, this study reported that Black females have a higher level of academic self-efficacy and hold a greater sense of the importance of completing a school year.

The question, then, is why? The article contributes the incredible dichotomy of Black male and female self-esteem factors to the notion that there are far fewer male elementary school teachers than female. So, at the time when minds are most thoroughly shaped, Black boys find themselves flailing in search of a positive, daily role model within the educational system. More often than not, the search comes up empty. Meanwhile, Black girls need look no further than their immediate teacher. For an alternate answer, Parham cites Dr. Jawanza Kunjufu, a Chicago educational consultant and author of the book *Countering the Conspiracy to Destroy Black Boys* and champion of the theory of the "Fourth Grade Failure Syndrome." Dr. Kunjufu stresses that, though the concept is certainly the catalyst, a lack of male role models at an early age is only one of many significant factors that contribute to the deterioration of the Black male ego. Without a positive male role model, a kind of vacuum of influence is created. As the young Black student's age increases, he is exposed to a heightened sense of peer pressure while simultaneously bearing witness to a significant shift in teaching styles (a shift for which he is grossly unprepared). As he enters high school, so decreases parental involvement in his daily life. So, as time passes in the young Black male's life, the adults that contribute most to his decisions grow fewer in number while the number of peers that influence his actions increases exponentially.

In order to shed light on this troubling matter, it would behoove us to take a look at the statistics surrounding what Dr. Kunjufu suggests to be the two most significant turning points in a young student's life: the fourth and eighth grade standardized tests.

Fourth and Eighth Grade Testing Results

For those unfamiliar with the process, the examinations thrust upon children in fourth and eighth grade assess a child's progress through his/her time in grammar school. It is widely assumed by a great many educators throughout the country that a child's entire academic future can be measured by his/her performance on the reading and mathematics portions of these exams. It is no secret, meanwhile, that the majority of children of color do not fare well on these tests.

Reports issued by the U.S. Department of Education in 2003 revealed several statistics of note. For one, the average reading scale score of our nation's fourth graders saw a rare improvement from 2000 to 2003. In addition, the average score of eighth graders was higher in 2003 than it was in 1992. In both the fourth and eighth grades, females outperformed males while White and Asian/Pacific Islander students had higher average scores than American Indian, Hispanic, and Black students. Turning to math, the average score for fourth and eighth graders was higher in 2003 than in all previous assessments. In both grades, it is interesting to note, males scored higher than females. Asian/Pacific Islanders scored higher than Whites, and both groups scored higher than American Indian, Hispanic, and Black students.

The reason that these figures are so intriguing to many scholars is that they seem to directly reflect common social constructs. It is also remarkable how closely the scores can be tied to dropout rates. In other words, many educators can (reasonably accurately) predict which students will wind up dropping out of school. From there, it is easy to determine which students will live below the poverty line. The poverty line is also typically an excellent indicator as to the kind of social desperation that leads to incarceration and/or welfare.

It isn't just the numbers that cause this trend, either. A poor grade alone could not possibly leverage a child into the kind of reckless path that these studies suggest. The real horror lies in how much weight is put onto the scores themselves. Rather than using them as an indicator for a child's needs, these numbers are employed to lump children into specific categories of student. Being improperly labeled as a fourth grader with 'special needs' amounts practically to a death sentence when it comes to educational achievement on the part of the child. And in eighth grade, with labels such as "Far Below Basic," "Basic," "Advanced" and "Advanced Placement" comes a significant hierarchy of social and educational stigma.

Detrimental Behavioral Patterns of Black and Hispanic Students

In addition to the alarming disparity of test scores compared to their White counterparts, the majority of children of color exhibit a few key behavioral patterns that trend towards failure. According to a 2003 study by the National Center for Education Statistics, Black and Hispanic children do not tend to spend their leisure time wisely. 17% of Black eighth graders and 13% of Hispanic eighth graders read for fun on a daily basis; numbers that are markedly lower than the 21% of White eighth graders and 27% of Asian/Pacific Islander eighth graders who read daily. Meanwhile, 32% of Black eighth graders and 17% of Hispanic eighth graders report watching 6 or more hours of television or videotapes each day.

Furthermore, children of color do not tend to adequately prepare for their future. As displayed by Table 3 below, in the year 2000, Black, Hispanic and American Indian/Native Alaskan students had the lowest percentage of high school graduates who completed advanced academic courses—or, in other words, took the extra steps necessary to be better prepared for college. Notice the difference in the numbers between children of color and White and Asian/Pacific Islander students. Across the board, the latter two groups lead by a significant margin.

Advanced Course—Taking in High School				
Students		**Courses**		
	Science	*Mathematics*	*English*	*Foreign Language*
Blacks	61%	32%	27%	20%
Hispanics	56%	31%	26%	31%
Whites	64%	47%	36%	31%
Asian/ Pacific Islander	80%	69%	40%	36%
American Indian/ Native Alaskan	43%	29%	27%	17%

Table 3

Black and Hispanic students also tend to score considerably lower on the Advanced Placement Exams than their White and Asian/Pacific Islander peers. As illustrated in Table 4 (a 2003 survey of Advanced Placement Exams statistics provided by the National Center for Education Statistics), Black and Hispanic high school students scored consistently below the national average on all four placement exams.

Advanced Placement Exams Average Scores				
Students		**Exams**		
	Calculus	*English Language & Comprehension*	*Chemistry*	*U.S. History*
Blacks	2.2	2.2	1.7	1.9
Hispanics	2.4	2.4	1.9	2.1
Whites	3.2	3.1	2.8	2.8
Asian/ Pacific Islander	3.2	3.1	2.9	2.8
American Indian/ Alaskan Native	2.5	2.6	1.9	2.3

Table 4

The sad truth is that the real preparation for the future tends to begin even before high school, where the statistics for children of color appear to be even worse. To illustrate, the National Research Council found that 37% of Asian American and 31% of White eighth graders planned to enroll in a college preparatory curriculum in high school. At the same time, 25% of Black eighth graders demonstrated college prep aspirations. The number drops further for Hispanic eighth graders, as they weigh in at 23%.

This lack of aspiration can be directly linked to both dropout rates and college enrollment rates among racial groups, as well. The National Council Report states that, in the year 2000, Hispanics accounted for 11% of all U.S. high school graduates. Only 7% of those same graduates went on to attend a four-year college or university.

Many would perhaps suggest that, owed to the kinds of numbers listed above, the teachers are to blame. Interestingly, there isn't quite the same gap between high-minority schools and more diverse schools when it comes to the sheer numbers of unqualified or under-qualified teachers working outside their fields of expertise. In order to get a better understanding of how teachers can impact the potential of our children, therefore, we must first take a look at how our impoverished schools are going about retaining quality educators.

Unqualified and Out-of-Field Teachers

No argument regarding a child's education would be complete without a strict examination of the minds that guide it. In response, consider several studies that point to how under-trained and under-staffed our schools tend to be in high-poverty areas. Richard Ingersoll, a Graduate School of Education (GSE) Associate Professor at the University of Pennsylvania and author of a report entitled "Why Do High Poverty Schools Have Difficulty Staffing Their Classrooms with Qualified Teachers?", posits that school staffing problems arise primarily from the fact that more and more qualified teachers are departing their posts long before retirement. Ingersoll's study suggests that the high turnover rate in impoverished schools can be associated with the notion that qualified teachers are under-compensated, offered inadequate support from school administrators, forced to contend with student discipline problems, and allowed limited input in school policymaking. Faced with a shortage of qualified teachers, high-poverty schools are then forced to take one or both of the following actions: Either they hire under-qualified teachers or move qualified and experienced teachers into a field in which they have no background.

With "How to Fix America's Schools", *Business Week Online* reveals the disturbing statistics associated with the former of the two actions. In a 1996 Tennessee study, fifth graders who had three years of effective instruction from a qualified teacher demonstrated an improvement in math scores to the tune of 83%. Only a 29% improvement was seen in students being taught by under-qualified teachers. This is especially alarming considering that the study also found that one third of all secondary school math teachers and roughly half of all physical science teachers didn't major or minor in the subjects that they were assigned to teach. The problem is magnified for largely minority schools, as well. As indicated by the *1999-2000 Public School and Public Charter School Survey* conducted by the U.S. Department of Education, students in high-minority schools were far more likely than students in low-minority schools to be taught English, Science and Mathematics by an out-of-field teacher.

This, of course, is not intended to be a rant on the qualities of the under-qualified teacher. In fact, many of these educators are truly noble people, taking the leftover jobs that nobody else wants in order to help impoverished schools meet their curriculum needs under a tight and constricting budget. Many times, these teachers are young people straight out of college who have entered the world of education in the hopes of making a difference for otherwise disadvantaged students. They work hard, and for that they should be commended. To stress, it is not the fault of these under-qualified or out-of-field teachers; it is the fault of the system.

The Overrepresentation of Minorities in Special Education Classes

In "Referring Language Minority Students to Special Education" (*ERIC Clearinghouse on Languages and Linguistics Digest*, 1991), author Paula Olson suggests that 12% of the language minority population in the U.S. may require special education. Given this statistic, in many school districts, language minority students are overrepresented in special education while, in other districts, and in certain categories of special education, there is an under-representation of handicapped language minority students. In other words, more Hispanic children who are unable to speak English well are being misdiagnosed and inappropriately placed into special educations classes while the children who really have speech impairments and lack the ability to function in a normal classroom are being held exempt. In a way, the stigma is derived more from a lack of understanding and proper pronunciation of the language than a lack of understanding of things like math and science, but the language barrier just isn't given enough credence.

In her article, "Reducing the Disproportionate Representation of Minority Students in Special Education" (*ERIC Clearinghouse on Disabilities and Gifted Education*, March 1998), author Jane Burnette states that, even though, in 1992, Black students accounted for only 16% of the total U.S. student population, they represented 32% of students in programs for mild retardation, 29% in programs for moderate mental retardation, and 24% in programs for serious emotional disturbance. These numbers remain in trend today.

According to the executive summary known as *Racial Inequality in Special Education* developed as part of the Civil Rights Project spearheaded by Harvard University in 2002, members of the study found that, in 1998, approximately 1.5 million minority children were identified as having mental retardation, emotional disturbance, or a specific learning disability. Of these 1.5 million children, 876,000 (or 58.4%) were Black or Native American. In most states, Black children were identified as one and a half to four times more likely to be placed into disability categories such as mental retardation and emotional disturbance. In addition, most of these same minority students were significantly more likely to be removed from the general education program and placed into a more restrictive environment. Finally, the study showed that Black and Latino students are about twice as likely as White students to be educated in such a setting.

The Role of the Church

So, with all these troubling numbers and trends looming, more questions than answers seem to emerge from the fog. Who will pick up the slack? Who is left to right the ship?

Of course, based on both the title of this segment and the title of this book, it is easy to see that I believe that the church has not taken on a prominent enough role. The fight surely remains a political one, but when looking at things through the looking glass that is the clergy, a new series of questions can also be raised. How can we overcome the bonds and hang-ups of religious differences and challenge Capitol Hill's take on how to deal with our struggling children of color? Since this is in no way a religious issue, can we, as a religious institution, separate the conditions of our faith from the shortcomings of public policy? How, in the face of the rocky past that was segregation and poorly planned integration, can we make schools truly fair?

The truth is that, these days, things aren't just about Black vs. White anymore. With the many outside influences assaulting our sons and daughters, the issue has become far more clouded. In response, the following chapters represent an attempt to uncover the many negatives that keep our children from achieving success and then move on to explaining exactly how the church can go about answering all of these questions.

CHAPTER 3

The Attitude:
Education as a Social Construct in the
Black Community

Many of our families have weathered the burden of the segregation of pre-Civil-Rights-era. America and all of us currently bear witness to the shortcomings of the equal–rights-fueled concept of integration. While the definition of inequality may have been abundantly clear during the early half of the 1900s, today, the lines have grown quite a bit more blurred. Untold numbers of influences that never would have faced Black children before have become so prevalent in modern times that they simply cannot be ignored. At least, not any longer.

The stance presented in this chapter is that Black children tend to be encouraged by their peers and cultural circumstances to hold back; to accept mediocrity or even failure. By removing common arguments like economic standing and racial prejudice from the discussion, a new kind of picture will emerge, one that demonstrates how critical self-identity is when it comes to the lagging efforts of Black children's test scores, graduation rates and overall academic performance. Considering the statistics demonstrated in the previous chapter, it is clear that the motivation to learn just isn't there anymore.

The questions raised by this viewpoint are many. Are intelligent Black children seeing their achievements ridiculed by their peers? In other words, has it become so un-cool to be smart that there is very little motivation to advance one's education in the first place? If so, where does this line of thinking come from? How has this undeniably rare cultural influence, one that suggests avoiding the betterment of self, developed over time?

Also, it will be critical to examine the plethora of alternate life avenues impressed upon young Black students. Can it be said that there is an inordinate amount of enticing "get-rich-quick" schemes presented to young Black American culture each day? Is the number of students in our communities who turn their backs on education in favor of earning fast money in the drug market growing as sharply as it would seem? Why is it that almost every young Black man seems to dream of a life in the rap game or professional sports? Have such lofty and perhaps misappropriated goals caused them, as a whole, to give up on the prospect of a decent education? Could it be that everything from the entertainers lauded by Black children to the clothing lines so popular in our communities has shaped this most troubling cultural value?

It is important to understand, however, that, while White America has served both historically and contemporarily as the measuring stick for Black youth, it is not culturally to blame for our children's lack of motivation. It is my firm belief that the attitude of self-debasement displayed by the majority of our children is less a retaliation against White culture than a misguided observation of self (an attempt to maintain and proudly define Black identity despite a political decree of equality).

Even if this chapter does manage to comprehensively answer all of the questions listed above, there are still many concerns left to explore. For example, how much of our children's tendency toward self-destructive behavior can be blamed on the frantic search for cultural identity? How is segregation and integration to blame for shaping the concept of the 'other' (or the systematic need to identify Black culture as something completely different from White culture)? And, finally (and most importantly), how has the church managed to perpetuate these attitudes over the years?

Dressing Like a Black Boy, Talking Like a White Boy

There is an odd sort of ridicule placed upon Black men and women who have managed to reach the plateau of higher education. Many entertainers, sports figures, sportscasters and even intellectual African Americans have been shunned by Black culture simply because they "sound too White." In other words, they "look Black" and "act Black," but just don't "sound Black." There are several rather intriguing points to consider about this sentiment. For one thing, "sounding White" seems to be tantamount to sounding educated. Where does this fear or rejection of the concept of speaking polysyllabically and with academic integrity come from? Another point is the idea that "sounding White" is so readily shunned by the community. Have Black men and women become so intent upon separating themselves from White culture that they cannot even accept the desire to compete on a similar intellectual level? And the final point is that "sounding Black" has been given such deep definition.

The lyrical rise and fall of Ebonics-influenced speech has become less a cultural indicator and more of a prerequisite of colored identity.

All of these influences seem to result in a rather odd sense of inner conflict for the young Black student. On the one hand, he/she is encouraged to celebrate his/her own culture and to be truly proud of his/her Black heritage (and there is absolutely nothing wrong with that, to be certain). On the other hand, however, he/she is also encouraged to shun anything labeled "too White," even when something carrying the label may actually benefit both him/her and his/her culture in the long run.

With "Racial Identity and Its Assessment in a Sample of African-American Men in Treatment for Cocaine Dependence" (*American Journal of Drug and Alcohol Abuse*, February 2000), researchers Jose M. Pena, Irma J. Bland, Denese Shervington, Janet C. Rice and Edward F. Foulks examine the effects of race identity on one of society's greatest pitfalls: drug dependency. While their sample pool and, for the most part, their polling results do not really relate to this particular study, their concepts on the shaping and execution of Black identity most certainly do. The authors' research has indicated that, "racial identity may be understood

> The lyrical rise and fall of Ebonics-influenced speech has become a prerequisite of colored identity.

and distinguished as that aspect of personal identity that specifically represents an individual's evolving awareness and adaptation to the consequences of being a visible person of color in a particular social context." Essentially, in order to lay the roots of one's cultural or personal identity, one must first take into account a whole range of physical attributes and social conditions. In addition, "racial identity theory predicts that, once the reality of racial status and its consequences have been confronted, many individuals enter a phase of identity development that involves idealization of their own racial group and devaluation of others. For African Americans, this phase is associated with idealized Black and anti-White attitudes."

This condition, of course, is based on a wide number of studies conducted by J.E. Helms in the early 90s through the present day, studies that both qualify racial identity as an evolving process and quantify the terms representative of the stages in that process. With their study, "Black Adolescent Girls: Do Gender Role and Racial Identity Impact Their Self-Esteem?" (Sex *Roles: A Journal of Research*, November 2005), authors Tamara R. Buckley and Robert T. Carter represent one of the first attempts to quantify the significance of the adolescent stage in shaping a Black child's gender, racial, and personal identity. This particular study is relevant for two reasons: One, it applies Helms' widely-accepted theory of racial identity, and two, it directly refers to the stage of development (adolescence) that most influences a child's decision to pursue or avoid the school system.

The study highlights Helms' theory of the four distinct statuses of racial identity development: pre-encounter, encounter, immersion-emersion, and internalization. According to Buckley and Carter's article, during the pre-encounter phase, "an individual depends on White society for self-definition and approval and exhibits negative attitudes toward his or her own racial group." For our purposes, this step refers to the development of a sense of the 'other', or the early stages of defining Black culture as something that is little more than non-White. The second step, (the encounter phase) "is characterized by psychological confusion and emotional turmoil triggered by an experience that challenges one's existing beliefs about the meaning and significance of race."

But the most intriguing views suggested by this study are categorized in the third and fourth steps. The former represents where I believe Black culture, as a whole, to be today while the latter represents the kind of utopian identity envisioned during the early phases of integration. In summary, the third step, immersion-emersion, refers to a period where the "individual attempts to discover his or her Black heritage by adopting a superficial and defensive Black identity, while idealizing Black culture, and denigrating White culture," and the fourth step, internalization, represents a shift in the direction of a "positive attitude toward members of [one's] own racial group as well as other racial groups." Only when this stage is achieved can social and political activism supplant the shortcomings of strict and segregated racial and cultural identities.

Buckley and Carter's article moves on to suggest that, during the adolescent phase, young Black girls (and boys, as the projection indicates), struggle a great deal with the concept of racial identity. Could it be that, in the absence of positive adult influences to demonstrate a more "internalized" view of what it means to be a proud Black citizen in America, children tend to turn to a more escapist method of shaping cultural and personal identity? Can it be inferred that, unless we take strides to teach our children what it means to be Black, they will resolve themselves to the erroneous notion that it means little more than being anti-White?

In answer to these questions, I invite the study of the emerging elements of Black youth culture. Even considering all of the above, it seems like a bit of a leap of faith to categorize children of color, as a whole, as struggling through the immersion-emersion status. In order to bridge the gap, it might be prudent to move away from the "he dresses like a Black boy, but talks like a White boy" argument and demonstrate how the immersion-emersion theory is represented in many common elements of Black pop culture.

FUBU and the Concept of Anti-Identity

To discover the common sentiments of Black youth today, look no further than the most popular line of apparel among the demographic. FUBU (an acronym widely understood

to stand for "For Us, By Us"), as a company, has grown exponentially since its founding in 1992, an act lauded on the
company website as initially representing a scheme for making
"easy money," as it were. Lately, the company has adopted
the slogan of "Enter Our World" and has ridden the back of
the intense popularity of all things distinctly Black and,
more importantly, distinctly non-White. The name of the
company itself, even if unintentionally, seems to carry a hint
of resentment towards White culture.

This kind of corporate thinking was embraced so readily
by Black youth that the phenomenon lead to the inception of
dozens of other clothing lines with similar separatist under-
pinnings. Enyce, along with its sister store, Lady Enyce,
features only Black models for all of its clothing. Rocawear,
a Roc-A-Fella Records-funded apparel line, touts itself as being
"at the forefront of hip hop's evolution into a borderless,
global lifestyle" and attributes its success to "becoming the
brand of choice for street-savvy…urban customer[s]."
Mecca's objectification of its female models for "Mecca
Femme" must be seen to be believed. And Phat Farm (with
its many subsidiaries), the brainchild of Russell Simmons,
claims to be a "brand born out of the hip hop lifestyle". Not
only does each line of clothing seem to pride itself on being
for Blacks only, they all are more than willing to embrace the
"hip hop lifestyle," one of the single greatest influences on
Black youth culture. And, in reality, young White America
has begun to feel the impact as well. These days, it is important
to recognize that the hip hop lifestyle is not so closely aligned

with racial boundaries. People from all races and religions have begun to embrace the culture.

For an example of how young Black students are lured away from the pursuit of education and toward a life of crime, violence, and "easy money," examine the lyrics of the self-proclaimed "CEO of the rap game," "New York's Ambassador," Jay-Z. Born Shawn Carter, Jay-Z has made his fortune in systematically climbing to the top of the rap charts (and as part owner of the New Jersey Nets.) En route, he founded his own record company and developed a wide range of products celebrating the street life, including the previously mentioned Rocawear. As he is considered the most popular rap artist operating today, his message speaks loudest to Black children.

> It is important to recognize that the hip hop lifestyle is not so closely aligned with racial boundaries.

Make no mistake, that message courses with lawless sentiments that include running drugs, objectifying women, killing White people (who are generally portrayed as the enemy or the 'devils'), and turning away from a reasonable living and taking to the streets, where the lifestyle is portrayed as an easy avenue to money, just so long as you don't get caught.

Even from his early albums, the message was clear. With the track entitled "D'Evils" (from *The Reasonable*

Doubt album, June 1996, Priority Records), Carter attempts to justify the lawless lifestyle with the lyrics, "Whoever said illegal was the easy way out couldn't understand the mechanics / And the workings of the underworld, granted / Nine to five is how to survive, I ain't trying to survive / I'm trying to live it to the limit and love it a lot / Life ills, poison my body / I used to say 'fu** mic skills,' and never prayed to God, I prayed to Gotti." On the same album, with "Coming of Age," via the accompaniment of Memphis Bleek, Carter portrays the true path to manhood for a young Black child: "He's sellin' weight, I'm sellin' eight balls / sixteen tryin' to graduate to pushin' quarters y'all." Certainly, an honest pursuit in the mind of a street dealer (at 16, the true coming-of-age, according to Carter), isn't pushing the books, it's pushing cocaine.

If our children are not getting proper counseling from teachers, parents, or even the church, it is only natural that they turn to the nearest figurehead for advice on how to shape their lives. With few responsible adults to support them, many young Black men and women are following the decrees of rappers like Jay-Z, who reminds them that, "Real niggaz do real things / On the road to riches and diamond rings / Real niggaz do real things / Bustin' my toast off the roof drinkin' 90 proof till spring" (from the *In My Lifetime, Vol. 1* album, November 1997, Roc-A-Fella Records). And, eventually, "The allure of breakin' the law / is always too much for [them] to ever ignore" (from *The Black Album* November 2003, Def Jam Records).

The truth is that, with so many new rap stars emerging every day, with every new face that gets up on the stage and proclaims how easy it is to make money in the rap game, the prospect of pursuing the thug lifestyle looks more and more appealing to the young Black student. Why spend 12 to 16 years studying when one can just step out on the streets, sell some rock cocaine, and make a fortune in a matter of months? Why go to college via the books when one can forgo college altogether and head straight to the NBA? As the data will show, an ever-increasing number of Black children are succumbing to this dangerous line of thinking.

The High Life

According to a recent study performed jointly by the Washington Post, The Kaiser Family Foundation, and Harvard University (Study conducted March 2006-April 2006), of the 1,328 African American men polled, many expressed optimism and self-blame for the problems facing young Black Americans, but also demonstrated some alarming responses regarding the growing rates of Blacks involved in violent crime, unemployment, and drug/alcohol abuse.

While it is certainly refreshing to see that 64% of Black men polled felt that the problems they face daily are the result of things that they have failed to do for themselves, the numbers regarding violent crime and drug use among peers are much more alarming. Eighty-nine percent said that the biggest problem facing young Black men is that they are not taking their education seriously enough. Eighty-seven percent cite drug and alcohol abuse while the same number suggests involvement in violent crime. Even more troubling is the notion that 74% of men polled claim that they have a close friend or family member who has been incarcerated at one point or another. Sixty-six percent know someone who has been murdered. More than one-fourth of those polled have been the victims of violent crime.

As part of the Washington Post's marvelous recent series entitled *Being a Black Man*, the article "Poll Reveals a Contradictory Portrait Shaded with Promise and Doubt" (*Washington Post*, June 4, 2006) by Steven A. Holmes and Richard Morin reflects on the findings of the aforementioned poll. According to Carl Bell, (President and CEO of the Community Mental Health Council and one of the experts cited in the article), part of the reason for this strange disparity in viewpoints is that Black men are so regularly subjected to conflicting images of their identity in pop culture. In addition to the cultural influences listed in the previous section, films like Curtis "50 Cent" Jackson's recent *Get Rich or Die Tryin'* breed a kind of "outside system putting [the] lens on Black people, especially Black men, that says 'toxic demon', and this lens is transmitted to the general public…You get Black people buying into it, and Black people saying we have no strengths, no redeeming qualities." Doug Ford, contract administrator for Florida's Department of Children and Families, suggests that the devastating effect of such images causes, "Black men [to be] victimized twice: once by acts of racism that are less frequent today but still too common, and then again by the self-doubts and suspicions that are the living legacy of more than 300 years of legal and de facto discrimination…For some Black men, such concerns are background noise that occasionally prompts a wince. But for others, these suspicions paralyze them into inaction, build barriers where none exist, and prevent them from seizing 'the real opportunities that are out there'."

The absence of vision toward these real opportunities seems to be leading more and more Black men to a life of systematic violence and drug-related crime and dependence. According to "Caught in the Cross-Fire," an October 14th article in the New *York Times* written by Richard G. Jones, in the town of Trenton, New Jersey alone, gang membership has risen, "to slightly more than 17,000 in 2005 from about 10,000 in 2000, and, by nearly all accounts, it continues to climb." The article goes on to cite that primarily Black gangs such as the Crips and Bloods, who have experienced similarly anomalous growth in major cities throughout America, are principally involved in drug dealing and trafficking. They are also responsible for nearly one half of the assault-and murder-related crime in the state of New York.

Even those children that do not pursue the fast-money lifestyle of gangbanging and drug-running seem to display an overwhelming desire to pursue an equally damaging and unattainable path to riches. In a 1998 article entitled "Blacks and Sports—Lifeline or Noose?," *San Francisco Chronicle* Staff

Writer Joan Ryan suggests that an alarming number of young Black males believe that their best avenue for advancement lies in training to become a professional athlete. As the article cites, it is no secret as to why. Black athletes are afforded an incredible amount of exposure in the media, owed to a wide range of statistical probabilities regarding Black participation and success in professional sports.

This isn't to say that Blacks should be ashamed of such remarkable athletic prowess. It just seems that the achievements are too celebrated; and the polls reflect this sentiment. "Not surprisingly, a recent study by Northeastern's Center for the Study of Sport in Society found that

> The real odds of a high school athlete playing in any pro sport are 10,000 to 1. Playing in the NBA is a 50,000 to 1 shot.

66 percent of African American males between the ages of 13 and 16 believed they could earn a living playing professional sports, more than double the percentage of White males." The truly discouraging aspect of this number is that two-thirds of young Black males seem to be putting all of their stock into highly improbable outcomes: "The real odds of a high school athlete playing in any pro sport are 10,000 to 1. Playing in the NBA is a 50,000 to 1 shot." These numbers are even starker considering the fact that they refer to the odds of any child, regardless of race, making it in a professional

sport. The odds are magnified when only Black children are considered.

So if it can be suggested that too many young Black students are pursuing dangerous, illegal, or unattainable life goals, what or who is to blame? How is it that so many Blacks have turned their backs on the school system while so many Whites have continued to put their faith in the sociological advancement that higher education represents? The answer is illuminated via a quick study of history.

The Silence of the Church

Has the church become too silent regarding all the gaps of influence on the young Black student? In response to this question, Chapter 4 examines the historical role of the church in communities of color and, through this historical study, a very troubling picture will come to light. Today, has the Black church become too marginalized to create any kind of positive role model for the average Black youth? With rap stars, professional athletes and other avenues of pop culture speaking so loudly, the lack of a true voice on the part of the church bears an unacceptable resemblance to tacit approval. If we don't take measures to stand up for and speak out on behalf of our failing children, we are as much to blame as the allure of easy money and drug-related violence.

As we will see, the Black church used to be a kind of forum for the concerned congregant to raise and address troubling neighborhood issues. There was a time when the church had a voice in the education of our youth. There was a time when the church served as the cultural, spiritual, and moral epicenter of each community of color. These days, however, discussion of social issues has either been pushed into the background or dismissed altogether. Without the discussion that we used to rely so heavily upon, the organization, as a unit, is essentially allowing this discouraging cycle of failure and violence to continue.

One group in Philadelphia offers the kind of outreach program that used to be left predominantly to the church. With an examination of what groups like Men United are doing, we can come to a better understanding of how to take a more proactive approach to protecting and bettering our children. Reporting for the *Philadelphia Weekly*, writer Kea Gregory chronicles the group's efforts to inject a more positive male presence into local communities. With "We Need the Men to Come Back," Gregory reveals how the members of Men United "raid drug-infested street corners, [and] come with job opportunities, GED programs, drug counseling, health services, and parenting workshops for the city's most marginalized residents." Men United co-chair Bilal Oayyum sums it up best when he says, "Basically, we're trying to say to these guys, 'You ain't got to be on the corner.'"

Meanwhile, in Sacramento, California, a league of religious institutions, both predominantly White and predominantly Black or Hispanic, have banded together to take on the issues at a scope that would be well beyond any single church in the area. Sacramento Area Congregations Together" (or Sacramento ACT) states on its website that they are "organizing to ensure that families live in safe neighborhoods, have access to affordable health care, good schools, and decent housing. Together, we can rebuild our communities and create an environment where families can live with dignity."

Among the group's most noteworthy efforts is the "Stand Together" campaign. This program saw the assembly of more than 500 community members and city officials hoping to create a kind of forum for discussing the issues surrounding youth and gang violence in the Sacramento area. With so many great minds in one place, ACT has managed to secure a four-fold plan of action to help right the wrongs of a struggling society.

The first step is known as "Early Intervention" and was put into place as recently as the fall of 2006. This agenda calls for a center of volunteers who focus on the growing concern over student truancy at local schools; after all, idle hands are the devil's workbench. This center promotes "positive follow-up services" that confront frequently truant students and their parents. The other arm of the Early Intervention program targets younger high school and middle school students that have demonstrated unacceptable scores on state-mandated aptitude tests. The hope is that building awareness and offering help will put these children on course for improvement before it is too late and they fall too far behind.

The second step in the "Stand Together" campaign calls for the strengthening of a local mentoring effort. Called "Caring Adults and Youth Mentors," this program looks to pair working individuals with high school and middle school students in need of a positive adult influence. The eventual goal is to turn the students into mentors; a goal that, should it come to fruition, would see high school seniors who have already traveled the hard road towards improvement begin to mentor middle school students. ACT believes that the best way to build the proper manpower for this kind of effort is to pursue a city policy that mandates release time for city workers who wish to be mentors. The hope here is that such a mandate would better and more fluidly pair the city's workforce with its schools.

The third arm of "Stand Together" is known as "Positive Alternatives." It looks to implement and expand "congregation-based tutoring and after-school programs." The thinking is that, with the backing of a caring coalition, even the most impoverished churches in the area can find the support and funding they need to improve their current educational outreach programs. Via the website (www.SacYouth.com), ACT hopes that beneficial ideas (and maybe even funding) can be funneled into some of the smaller programs wither larger aspirations.

And the fourth program of "Stand Together" calls for a greater realm of career exposure for young people who are still in school. A kind of task force has been created by ACT, one that will focus "on increasing summer jobs for youth and student internships. Currently, the Sacramento community has only fragmented efforts to create jobs for youth." The hope, in this case, is that ACT, through its tireless volunteer efforts, can work to fill in the gaps between these "fragmented efforts."

Conclusion

The efforts of groups such as Sacramento ACT are certainly noble ones. The city of Sacramento surely will become a better place as a result of this group's endeavors. But thinking in terms of a city on its own is perhaps not a wide enough scope. In Sacramento, there are already "fragmented efforts" to improve youth participation and performance in local schools, and this certainly holds true for almost every major American city (and many small ones, too). All over the country, there are pockets of the kinds of agendas that this book promotes. What we are missing is a national agenda, a centralized call to action.

Without such an action, the initiative is divided and, therefore, far less effective. As such, many of our children are essentially left to their own devices. And, through an odd combination of a misplaced and misrepresented sense of identity, the barrage of negative Black images on the part of the American media machine, and the vacuum of positive leadership presented by the Black church, most boys and girls of color find themselves failing of their own volition.

In summary, if we continue to put so much stock in sociological disadvantages, racism, fast-money, and "street creed," without offering cohesive alternative solutions to rise above the disadvantages placed upon Black people, we continue to feed the fires of our culture's most grievous shortcomings. The Black church, as a whole (and regardless of sectarian affiliation) has failed to help its children come to a better understanding of what the struggle is in the first place. As a highly-attended and well-funded church demographic, there is absolutely no reason why we cannot sponsor outreach programs similar to Men United or Sacramento ACT. But that isn't really the point, either. The point is that a national agenda needs to be realized; that way, it will not matter if you live in Sacramento, New Orleans, or New York. The question, then, is where is this national agenda? And, more importantly, since we have not managed to build a cohesive effort against the problem, what message are we sending to our children?

PART TWO

The History

History, despite its wrenching pain, cannot be unlived, but if faced with courage, need not be lived again.

—*Maya Angelou*

CHAPTER 4

The Historical Role of the Black Church

If it can be stated that the cultural mold of segregation and the catalysis of integration has led to a rather destructive sense of self-identity in the consciousness of most students of color, then several questions arise. Not least among them is the question of why. It is my belief that things were so different for children of color during the Civil Rights era, not just because of the sweeping, intrepid attitude of that particular parent generation, but because of the autonomy that segregation afforded, as well. This is not to say that I condone the concept of segregation; certainly, it was an antiquated idea born of racism that bore very little quality on the health of a student's level of acceptance and understanding. It is just that I see its value when taken against the backdrop of cultural identity.

Like it or not, the simple truth about segregation is that, by nature, it was about defining things; about defining people. At the heart of the debate, and serving as roots for the construct itself, was the specific definition of Black and White identity. Essentially, everything from public bathrooms to cultural tendencies was carefully categorized. Though they may well have been forced upon people, at the very least, identities were clean-cut. Outside the school, of course, things were very troubling for a Black man or woman in those days, but while at school, there was at least relatively little cultural and personal insecurity on the part of the Black student, who often found him/herself surrounded by people with similar values, beliefs, and ideals.

I do not pretend to ignore the fact that there was a great deal of anti-White sentiment even then. Certainly, a case can be made for the idea that people of color resented White culture even more in those days than they do now. That is not in question here. What is in question is whether or not there is a measurable discrepancy between Black pride in the Civil Rights era and Black pride today.

Obviously, as discussed in the previous chapter, there are any number of cultural influences that plague the hearts and minds of young Black America. I am of the opinion, however, that the roots of these influences can be traced to the birth of integration.

> Today integration seems to suggest a need for all cultures creeds and religions to blend together as one.

At its outset, integration was supposed to be about fairness (and rightfully so). The drafters of its regulations imagined a kind of utopian harmony between Black and White students, albeit the reality of a distant future. But, somewhere along the line, the values that shaped the concept were misconstrued. What was meant to be a system that celebrated and encouraged diversity has, in fact, become a system that challenges unique cultural beliefs. Today, integration seems to suggest a need for all cultures, creeds, and religions to blend together as one; that no man or woman is lesser than another and, as such, every man or woman is required to act like everyone else.

The truth of the matter is that integration is not going anywhere anytime soon. And, since there does not seem to be any viable replacement, save for taking a step back in cultural advancement by embracing segregation once again, there is nothing left for Black America but to attempt to regain the kind of pride and identity celebrated by the generations that came before us. In other words, we, as a culture of color, need to rediscover what is right for us. In this modern PC age, we want fairness, to be certain; but not at the cost of our own voice. We need to come to terms with the fact that we have to be neither White nor anti-White in order to be a successful cross-section of American society. Integration should not be taken as it has been. Integration should not appear to our children as a kind of tool to make everyone just a little more White. Rather, it should be viewed in a different light: one that suggests to children of color that they need to celebrate their cultural values and show a little pride in the face of adversity. The health of African Americans everywhere, to say nothing of the health of the school system—would do well to embrace integration in its purest sense; in the sense that it is the application of diversity, rather than conformity.

> We need to come to terms with the fact that we have to be neither White nor anti-White in order to be successful.

But the question of whether we, as a culture, lack the true sense of pride and identity demonstrated by our parents and grandparents remains unanswered. Had polls such as the one conducted by the *Washington Post*, the Kaiser Family Foundation, and Harvard University (cited in Chapter 3) existed during the Civil Rights era, this question would be met with a prepackaged answer. In the absence of true data, however, an examination of history (particularly, for our purposes, the history of the Black church) is in order.

Since this book aims to demonstrate that the Black church can and should carry more bearing on the social and educational health of its congregants, before delving into its history, it would be prudent to demonstrate a connection between religion and racial identity. To that end, I would like to draw attention to an article entitled "Exploring the Relationship Between Racial Identity and Religious Orientation Among African American College Students," by Delida Sanchez and Robert T Carter (*Journal of College Student Development*, May/June 2005). With the article, the authors not only suggest that religion carries significant weight on the prospect of identity development (particularly in the minds of adolescent and college-age students), but that it carries the most weight for African Americans, as well. While it can be stated that White values are also greatly influenced by religious background, "For people of African decent, religious beliefs and practices have and continue to be a salient aspect of culture and upbringing…Religious denominations provide frameworks from which to practice specific beliefs, rituals, and rites. These frameworks encompass empowering ideologies about family and communal unity, shared values, and life style behaviors."

With this chapter, I intend to demonstrate that the true shortcomings of integration do not arise from the construct itself, but rather, from our reaction to the construct. Without the influence of positive role models, students of color are left to examine what integration means on their own. As demonstrated in Chapter 3, that kind of situation has managed to lead our children down a dangerous path. Integration is not at fault here. What is at fault is the lack of that necessary framework. There is a gap in leadership that occurs somewhere between the school and the home—one that, as Wikipedia suggests, has historically been bridged by the Black church: "The Black church likewise filled the void created by the lack of any meaningful political role for blacks in either the segregated South or much of the North in the first half of the twentieth century." Gone are the days when "the Black church served not only as a place of worship, but also as a community 'bulletin board,' a credit union, and a 'people's court' to solve disputes."

Gone, also, is the period where the Black church enjoyed its greatest sense of strength within its surrounding neighborhood. There was a kind of activist pride that used to exist among a congregation. Pastors and pastoral groups took a stance on the educational, political, and social health of their parishioners, well-supported community outreach programs were commonplace (and often produced significant results) and religion, regardless of sectarian affiliation played a viable and highly visible role in the shaping of cultural values. To demonstrate, I offer the following historical reflection on the role of the Black church.

An Activist History

In their famous book, *The Black Church in the African American Experience*, C. Eric Lincoln and Lawrence H. Mamiya posit that, "The impact of the Black church on the spiritual, social, economic, educational, and political interests that structure life in America—including mainline White churches themselves—can scarcely be overlooked in any realistic appraisal of our common religious experiences." Indeed, the birth of the Civil Rights movement marked the period where Black church activism was at its height, but it certainly was not where it laid its roots. If statements like Lincoln and Mimiya's can be made confidently, then it must also be suggested that the trend can be traced all the way back to the origins of Black faith. For our purposes, however, an examination of the church from the early 1900s through the landmark case of Brown vs. Board of Education would be prudent.

In the 1930s and 40s, we see the first significant emergence of religious belief dictating social reform and activist movement. Among the sects were the Universal Peace Mission Movement, the United House of Prayer for all People, the Gospel Spreading Church of God, and the Nation of Islam.

There are several interesting elements concerning these religious movements. The first is that they were all lead by men or women who had been lofted to the height of near-deity. In fact, many of these leaders were openly exalted as a kind of Black Messiah. The second item of interest surrounding these groups is that they were formed during a period that, as far as Blacks are concerned, closely parallels today's economic structure. As the economic separation between poor, urban Black people and affluent Black congregants grows wider, the figureheads that would lead religious change grow stronger, and the more likely it is for other sectarian movements to spring up. Most of these groups enjoyed wild popularity during the times of greatest economic concern for minority people. These days, many of them have grown somewhat obsolete, with the exception of the Nation of Islam.

That the Nation of Islam is the most prevalent remaining separatist sect speaks to the fact that it has enjoyed a long history of powerful leadership. Another powerful testament to its longevity is owed to the notion that, at its outset, it was billed as a movement dedicated to resurrecting all aspects of daily life (the economic, spiritual, social, and mental conditions) for Black men and women in both America and abroad. Its current national leader, the Honorable Minister Louis Farrakhan, has managed to uphold and advance the group's remarkable efforts to improve impoverished neighborhoods, reform the criminal element, and encourage self-respect and independence among Black people everywhere. Of course, Farrakhan's most notable effort regarding Black empowerment was the coordination of the Million Man March in Washington DC on October 16, 1995, arguably the most significant representation of Black pride and solidarity since the Civil

Rights era. The event, conceived as an effort to get more Black men to vote and get involved with volunteer work and community activism, achieved exactly what it sought to achieve, as well. Voter registration and volunteerism rose sharply among the Black male demographic in the months following the demonstration.

But the Million Man March was simply a drop in the pail when compared to the decades-long movement that preceded it. Beginning in 1954 with Brown vs. Board of Education and spanning until approximately 1980, a generation of people headed and supported the proudest period in Black history, the Civil Rights movement.

Many scholars equate this landmark period with the church itself. Serving as the most natural avenue for congregants to exercise the kind of leadership that the society of the day had denied them, Black churches naturally developed a substantial number of leaders within the realm of social reform. Clergymen, in those days, held a far more influential role, and some of them went on to the kind of notoriety not often reserved for American church leaders. The most famous of these men was the figurehead for the Civil Rights movement itself, Dr. Martin Luther King, Jr. The 1964 Man of the Year (*Time Magazine*) and Nobel Peace Prize winner got his start as Pastor of the Ebenezer Baptist Church in Atlanta. While his mark on modern American society is unmatched, he was merely one of many notable Civil Rights activists who began their careers in the ministry. Lost in the shuffle of history are the efforts of great clergymen like C.T. Vivian, Bernard Lee,

Ralph Abernathy and Fred Shuttlesworth. All of them found their first true religious and political podiums within the walls of their respective churches.

Brown vs. Board of Education not only represented the first true victory of the Civil Rights movement in 1954, it led to one of the most significant factors in the shaping of Black student identity, as well. It is well understood that the case was first heard on the basis of a strike by 117 Black high school students expected to attend the dilapidated, segregated Moton High. It is less often discussed, however, that Barbara Johns, the student strike leader, was influenced by her father Vernon Johns and other current and former leaders of the Dexter Street Baptist Church. Prior to the strike, opinions among Black community members were divided on whether or not to take action against the institution of segregation and all the financial and educational shortcomings that it represented. The unifying effort was spearheaded by the Reverend Francis Griffin, who used his position as both church leader and President of the local NAACP to voice his opinion on the matter at every turn. Eventually, the Reverend convinced the PTA of Topeka middle and high schools in Topeka, Kansas to take action

> Brown vs. Board of Education led to one of the most significant factors in the shaping of Black student identity.

on the matter and request the kind of educational reform that led to the landmark hearing.

But this case was not necessarily the catalyst that led to great change. The entire Civil Rights movement, as is well known, was sparked by the courage of Rosa Parks and the Montgomery Bus Boycott that her resolve engendered. What many do not realize, however, is that the Black church was instrumental in orchestrating its eventual success. Jo Ann Robinson, Professor of English at Alabama State College (a local Black university), created thousands of flyers announcing the December 5, 1955 boycott of the Montgomery public transportation system. The action (and the boycott itself) never would have reached fruition, however, had it not been for the efforts of local Black ministers and their churches. Since the boycott was to take place on a Monday, across the board, every local minister volunteered to announce the boycott to their congregations on the preceding Sunday. Once the boycott was found to be a success, many of these same ministers went on to form an organization known as the Montgomery Improvement Association (MIA), a group that would champion the cause of advancing Black rights in the region. Dr. King (then Pastor of the Dexter

The Black church was instrumental in orchestrating the eventual success of the Civil Rights movement.

Avenue Baptist Church) was of course selected as the president of the organization.

The evening of that December 5th highlights what is potentially the greatest moment in the history of the Black church. At the very least, it marks the moment when the church held its most influential role. The night of the landmark boycott, the new leaders of the MIA found that they needed a meeting place to help rally the cause that they felt to be emerging. The meeting place, as it turned out, was the Holt Street Baptist Church. Thousands gathered within its walls, which provided the perfect forum for people to voice their opinions and drive up interest in the future of the protest.

So, as it has been established that the church carried such a significant role in the proud history of Black America, before drawing any conclusions about whether the church could do more, it would behoove us to examine the current state of religion-fueled activism. Only in determining the ground upon which we stand today can we hope to elevate it in the future.

Sectarian Church Involvement

These days, as it was during the Civil Rights era, the church finds itself divided into various religious sects. The only difference between now and that most notable period in Black history is that these sects lack an all-encompassing goal like Civil Rights to unify their efforts. While it is true that many Baptist, Methodist, and Pentecostal churches (to name a few) continue to reach out their hands to the needs of suffering children of color all across America, without a centralized initiative, the plan remains a little piecemeal and, therefore, less effective than it would be otherwise.

While the Civil Rights effort, in many ways, still wages, we have borne witness to an unacceptable lag on the part of students of color. Since children so clearly shoulder the future of our culture in this nation, we must work to unify in the fight against this common front.

> Without a centralized initiative, the plan remains a piecemeal and, therefore, less effective than it would be otherwise.

But despite the lack of a national educational outreach effort, it is important to highlight the successes enjoyed by several charitable groups. Perhaps, if we all come to a better understanding of their goals and noble causes, we can identify broader methods to institute sweeping change to social, political, and (particularly) educational reform for poor minority communities.

In "The Role of the Black Church In Working With Black Adolescents" (*Adolescence*, Summer 1994), Roger H. Rubin, Andrew Billingsley, and Cleopatra Howard Caldwell elaborate on a study conducted on 176 Black churches from all across

America. Of the urban and rural churches polled, almost all of them boasted a community outreach program of some kind. The study revealed that, out of the cross-section of churches polled, 39% offered teen support programs, 31% offered sports activities, 16% provided funding for college, 15% focused on substance abuse programs and parenting issues, 8% sought to provide a positive role model and 3% worked to fight AIDS. Unfortunately, what is evident is that many of the programs that were set forth weren't conducted in conjunction with neighboring cities. All of these otherwise effective programs were done in isolation.

Zeroing in on one such program, in New York, Reverend Floyd H. Flake (a former Congressman who leads the Allen A.M.E. Church), has spurred his 8,000 member congregation into raising millions of dollars and volunteering thousands of hours to the redevelopment of the Queens community that surrounds it. Rev. Flake also founded the Shekinah Youth Chapel, a youth outreach program that provides faith-based instruction and worship services to troubled children and teens in one of the most crime- and drug-infested neighborhoods in all of New York: Jamaica Queens.

In Austin, Texas, we find a non-denominational effort that hopes to band local Black churches together to help combat the spread of AIDS within the community. The goals of the Black Church Outreach Project are to "allow Black church resources to inform, educate, and empower the community with respect to HIV/AIDS health issues; Mobilize community partnerships between Black churches and other community organizations," and "Link individuals who have a need for community and personal health services to appropriate community and private Black church providers."

So, what is the trouble with all of these programs? Nothing. It is just that their focus could be a bit broader. One provides aid to New York's impoverished minority children. Another (rightfully) centers on a non-denominational, church-based approach to combating AIDS, but focuses only on the needs of Austin. Hundreds more provide support to troubled teens or financing for impoverished high school children to attend college.

The true problem at hand, however, is that there are too many Black communities throughout the country that are in desperate need of rebuilding and refurbishing (not just in Queens, New York). AIDS afflicts our children outside the city limits of Austin just as frequently as inside. Teen support programs are needed in places other than St. Louis, Missouri and Trenton, New Jersey. Where are the multi-denominational, religious leader spearheaded programs that were so common in the 50s and 60s? Why must we divide our goals so readily? Where have our cohesive, centralized dreams gone?

The Church as Catalyst

It is not that churches of color have strayed very far from their historical role as the cultural and social hub of minority communities; the programs highlighted above would attest to the opposite. It is just that they seem to lack the kind of coordinated, unified approach necessary for exacting change. These days, too little emphasis is placed upon common goals that could unify otherwise sectarian values toward a common good. Institutions that find cause to disagree on faith-based matters should be willing to work together on earthly ones. And the leaders of these institutions should be prepared to put these differences aside in the name of a brighter future— as their predecessors once did during the Civil Rights era.

With "What Does It Mean to See a Black Church Burning? Understanding the Significance of Constitution-alizing Hate Speech" (*University of Pennsylvania Journal of Constitutional Law*, 1998), Michele M. Simmsparris intrepidly points out that "despite the presence of myriad factions of Black churches in America, the depiction of the monolithic Black Church is pervasive throughout African-American historiography as a matter of historical course." She goes on to say, however, that "In essence, the term 'the Black Church' is a misnomer. The term...implies that all Black churches share or have shared the same aspirations and strategies for creating cohesive African-American communi-ties. This is far from true." Far from true, indeed. Black churches, these days, are every bit as unique as the commu-nities that surround them. The only trouble is that, lately, they seem to have allowed their differences to outweigh their similarities when it comes to the task of unifying on behalf of minorities everywhere.

During the 50s and 60s, it was not at all uncommon for Baptist and Methodist churches, for example, to work together on social change. The significance of the goal of desegregation knew no religious boundaries. Whether it had been a Baptist church in Birmingham, Alabama or a Methodist church in Meridian, Mississippi that was burned to the ground did not matter. Despite the wild variation in political, religious, and ideological outlook, Black churches in every community rallied together to exact swift and aggressive legal reform.

In the eyes of modern religious leaders, therefore, the portion of the message decreed by Dr. King in arguably the most famous speech in American history seems to have been lost, when he called upon "all of God's children, Black men and White men, Jews and Gentiles, Protestants and Catholics," to join together in the pursuit of freedom. Note that, with this statement, Dr. King specifically invokes religion to stir social change, but most importantly, he calls for all men and women, regardless of color or creed, to band together in the cause of freedom and justice. Note, specifically, that he never once uses the term Baptist or Methodist. He never once mentions a religious sect more specific than the Catholic or Protestant faith. So, before moving on to the next chapter, ask yourself two questions: Have our churches done enough to keep Dr. King's dream of religious and social unity alive? And is there anything we can do, as a greater church body, to rally our Black congregants to take action and improve our communities and schools?

CHAPTER 5

No Child Left Behind:
Have Churches of Color Upheld
Their End of the Bargain?

To many, the concept of the Bush Administration's sweeping agenda known as No Child Left Behind represents the long-sought-after answer to our nation's decades-old struggle with raising educational standards. To others, it is simply another step in the evolving legislative battle that began with the Elementary and Secondary Education Act of 1965. To still others, it is an empty agenda, one based entirely upon campaign lip service, that calls for the same song and dance, cleverly disguised with a new name and perceived outlook.

While No Child Left Behind is an excellent and arguably groundbreaking agenda in theory and on paper, the numbers do not lie. As demonstrated in Chapter 2, children of color all across America are still grossly underperforming on their state-mandated tests, particularly in the areas of reading and math (two of the most specific weak points that this legislation attempts to address). So, the question then becomes, if we have state-supported and federally-funded mandates on the table, why don't they seem to be affecting any kind of real change for children of color?

The sad truth is that No Child Left Behind is not the first measure of its type. In fact, given the data presently at hand, it seems to be little more than another notch in the national rhetoric; another empty slogan in a long line of empty slogans. Whether the shortfalls of these programs are due to a lack of funding or support on the part of the administrations themselves or to the constant flux of the American presidency is up for debate, but the fact remains that there *are* failures—and, as such, they are worth talking about. What is more, we need to ask ourselves if, in the future, pointing fingers at the legislation is really worth the trouble.

Like former President Reagan's mandate regarding "A Nation at Risk," almost four years after its inception, No Child Left Behind seems to have made very little difference when it comes to the hard and fast numbers. As was the case with his father before him (a man who vowed to be remembered as the "Education President"), President George W. Bush seems to have lately turned his attention to the more immediate needs of a war in Iraq. Meanwhile, the promise of increased funding for America's schools has (arguably) run its course almost completely unfulfilled. The truly distressing aspect of this common and historical American problem, however, is that it doesn't even seem to be a partisan issue. Both major parties have demonstrated a desire (however hollow) to improve America's educational program. Former President Bill Clinton, with his six unprecedented education acts (Goals 2000: Educate America Act, the School-to-Work Opportunities Act, the Student Loan Reform Act, the Safe Schools Act, the National Service Trust Act, and the reformed version of the Elementary and Secondary Education Act of 1965) saw his efforts fail to bridge the substantial achievement gap as well.

I posit that regardless of the name given to the agenda, regardless of the broad, sweeping reform that a President may promise, this traditionally top-down approach to educational reorganization simply does not work. For anyone who does not agree, I invite an examination of the history of American education since that landmark act of 1965. Not only have reading, math, and science scores failed to significantly improve since that fateful year, in many districts and with many demographics, they have demonstrated a marked decline. In short, too many children of color continue to lag behind.

If we examine the promises made to America from the Reagan administration right on through the current Bush administration, it is easy to see that the answer is not a mandate. The answer, perhaps, is to create a road map. In other words, giving American educators an initiative without providing directives is tantamount to placing someone blindfolded in the middle of a cornfield and telling them to find the road. But before making such a claim, it is important that we evaluate some of the perceived strengths and weaknesses of No Child Left Behind.

NCLB: Pros and Cons

With its 2005 *Policy Brief: The NCLB Debate*, the University of Arkansas' Office for Education Policy attempts to take a bipartisan approach to summarizing the value of this infamous agenda. With the brief, the University sets out to determine whether "NCLB [will] have a revolutionary impact on America's schools." The measure for such "revolutionary impact" seems to be funding, whether teachers will feel empowered or "demoralized," and whether NCLB properly addresses the disparity between the educational performances of minority and White children. Rather than focusing on the polar arguments represented by this article, I will present its stated strengths and weaknesses on the part of this most controversial measure.

NCLB Strengths:
- That the public has ultimately been held accountable for the shortcomings of its students.
- Literacy has finally been recognized for the important educational and social factor that it is.
- In theory, NCLB will offer more support to the children of color who have traditionally lagged behind in academic performance.
- In centering on the importance of state test scores, the mandate has institutionalized the broader definition of success or failure.

NCLB Failures:
- According to a recent Government Accounting Office report, NCLB seems to be at least marginally under-funded.
- Yearly test scores do not properly assess a child's overall academic progress. Rather, it just demonstrates a child's ability to absorb large amounts of test-related information in the weeks leading up to the state tests.

Of course, these strengths and weaknesses do not account for the entire picture. In the section that follows, you will find several additional perspectives on where NCLB has fallen short.

An Administrative Mixed Bag

The existence of the kinds of successes and failures listed above is no surprise. It would be foolish to suggest that not every form of national policy has both its pros and cons. For NCLB, the new standards for teacher qualification, for example, are a huge step in the right direction. At the heart of the measure, too, we find a pure initiative; one that calls directly for the improvement of the test scores of America's children. In addition, there are a great number of schools in America that seem to have improved dramatically (both academically and physically) since the implementation of this most recent educational reformation. And, as stated by Eric Earling in his 2004 letter to the editor that appeared in the Moscow (ID) Daily News, "States voluntarily choose to participate in [No Child Left Behind]. In return for increased funding and flexibility, states are asked to be more accountable in showing the public that federal tax dollars are being used to improve student achievement—that's common sense."

Common sense, indeed. And while a handful of American states managed to demonstrate an improvement in test scores a year after Earling's letter, the nation as a whole remains in crisis. Part of the trouble with singing the praises of NCLB is that, since it is a state-level initiative, data can be culled from one state to demonstrate an improvement in reading scores, while data from another state can be examined to highlight a heightened effort toward the improvement of teacher accountability.

When all of this scattered data and partisan rhetoric is parted, however, we can begin to examine the national report card, so to speak. Over the past three years, it has become painfully obvious that NCLB has done little to close the achievement gap. Not enough consideration has been given to the fact that Black and Brown kids all across America (save for a few urban settings) are continuing to score significantly lower than their White and Asian counterparts. In fact, the breakdown of performance by race isn't even given a second thought when many educators, politicians, and pundits praise the across-the-board improvement of various integrated schools.

On the other hand, at the heart of the matter, there isn't enough support for how the legislation should be carried out on a daily basis. In other words, the government has granted stock answers to schools with unique problems. The states, educators, parents, and students of this country now have a better idea of what they need to do to succeed in the American educational system and for that, No Child Left Behind should be applauded. Very little consideration seems to have been given to *how* these same states, educators, parents, and children need to go about finding that success, however. Suggesting and then funding an initiative designed to improve the performance of our students without specifically explaining *how to improve* is tantamount to telling someone that they need to save at least $8,000-$10,000 every year but then forgetting to reveal the methods for doing so. Everyone knows that saving more money is a good idea, just like everyone knows that the United States is falling behind other developed countries in its educational performance. The question is not whether we need to meet these goals; the question is, how do we meet them on a day-to-day basis?

In addition to the notion that NCLB only attempts to answer stock questions (at least in the mind of Robin Ann Martin, Ph.D., who, with her 2004 article entitled "An Essay about No Child Left Behind" posited that the initiative needs to realign its focus), it seems to be asking the wrong questions to begin with. According to Dr. Martin, the most critical queries are the following four:

- How can schools better monitor themselves to create more fair and equitable instruction for children from all socio-economic levels?
- How can teachers be better educated about their own biases so that they become more willing to try out new approaches for multi-cultural strategies that engage children from diverse backgrounds?
- How can teachers come to "read" the signs of what "engaged learning" looks like in the day-to-day non-verbal clues of each child, so that the instruction is not so biased toward middle-class White children?
- How can teachers feel safe enough to question their own practices at a deeper level that brings about this kind of learning?

While the unanswered (or even unconsidered) questions are many, the final and potentially most alarming aspect of No Child Left Behind seems to go largely unnoticed by those who would argue for or against it: this latest initiative is slated well into the future. The current administration has suggested that we will not see the end result of NCLB across the board until we examine the surveyed numbers in the year 2014. While the idea that this problem has been decades in the making seems to render this time frame legitimate, the simple fact of the matter is that, in 2014, the U.S. will be headed by a different administration, or perhaps even a different political party; one that is sure to present its own catchy slogan, adding to the long line of catchy slogans that came before it. By then, the group that injected this act into the national consciousness will be well beyond accountability. As such, how much effort is really put into meeting the goal of a 100% passing rate among America's schools?

Since the true effectiveness and liability of this agenda cannot possibly be measured until it has had more time to develop and take root, it would be prudent to examine the best way to ensure that it does not fail. It is not my intention to suggest that NCLB is without value. In fact, I feel that it represents more room for potential than it does for failure. It is more than just a revision of "A Nation at Risk." It is more than an empty initiative, but only if we, as a concerned people, take action to make it better and demonstrate the kind of steadfast resolve it takes to see a national strategy through to the finish, as well.

How to Fill the Gaps

The primary question then is whether or not the church has done enough to support No Child Left Behind. The answer, it appears, is "no." There seems to be a great deal more that the vast numbers of minority neighborhood churches and Mega-Churches can do to ensure that the noble goals of NCLB do not leave us in the dust.

> Thousands of Black churches are falling behind on their *own* understanding of public education; their *Public Education IQ* has dropped below the acceptable range.

A unified front is clearly more effective when it comes to the prospect of broadly addressing the problems our children face. The true and immediate need for better and more focused outreach programs is also quite clear. What has not yet been discussed, however, is *why* all of these shortcomings have come to pass.

Simply put, the thousands of Black churches in America, when considered from an institutional standpoint, are falling behind on their *own* understanding of public education; their *Public Education IQ* has dropped below the acceptable range. It is not that the congregants of these honorable houses of worship do not want to improve themselves or their children (there is a reason they attend Sunday services in the first place, after all); it is that the churches themselves boast a Public Education IQ that has plenty of room for improvement. Not only do we not discuss topics like No Child Left Behind, we don't seem to know everything we can *about* them, either.

When is the last time that, within the walls of a church, you heard a preacher discuss the importance of not only raising our children's test scores, but of learning the significance of those test scores, as well? The reason may not necessarily be a lack of *desire* to talk about such hot-button issues; it may actually be a lack of *understanding* that emits from the pulpit. If we, as church leaders and church goers, took responsibility for raising our own Public Education IQ by studying up on the matters regarding our state's standardized tests, for example, we would have all the tools necessary to help our own children succeed (the very children who attend our churches year in and year out) even in the absence of a qualified or even caring teacher.

In other words, before we can truly teach, before we can truly improve, there is much to learn. We have to come to a greater understanding about the significance of the achievement gap before we can devise and demonstrate the best way to eliminate it. For example, we must learn everything there is to know *about* the high school exit exams in our districts before we can explain to our children the methods to achieving the best score, even from our own pulpit.

The only way to do the kinds of things listed above is to band together, as a church and open a dialogue with local legislators and educators. As a unit, we need to get the goods on the most pressing material facing our children. We need to let our congressmen and women know exactly how NCLB is failing us if we ever hope to see it succeed. In the process, we may just find it easier to take charge of our own educational destiny than we ever thought possible. At the very least, taking this kind of action boasts one very positive potential outcome; we will ensure that the next version of education initiative takes our struggling children of color into greater consideration.

The underlying message here is that solving our national education deficit isn't about policymaking. It isn't about socioeconomic conditions. It isn't about funneling more money into solving the problem. It is about *belief systems.* And, until we, as a nation and as a unified church, embark upon a calculated effort to discuss these belief systems and how they relate to education, in the future, we will continue to be greeted with the same shallow and shortsighted pacifiers that every presidential candidate in the history of the American educational system has managed to invent.

CHAPTER 6

An Aggressive Agenda:
The Empowerment Approach of the
Mormon Church

Chapter 5 closed with a call to arms of sorts; a careful and honest recommendation that the church take a more proactive stance when it comes to improving our children's outlook by building on its own Public Education IQ. Of course, it would be folly to present all of the recommendations that I have made within these pages (unifying our goals, opening dialogue, learning, taking action) without also offering an example of what this kind of agenda achieves. Fortunately, there is a church body in America that has historically confirmed the benefits of the kind of unified, education-conscious approach to which I have so often referred. What is more, the children of this church have demonstrated an enviable track record of success in the classroom as well as the 'real world'.

I am speaking, of course, of the Mormon Church (or more appropriately referred to as the Church of Jesus Christ of Latter-day Saints), a highly unified institution whose congregants not only boast remarkable performance on NCLB-mandated test scores, but serves as the perfect example of the kind of positive change that can be affected if a church, school, or university takes strides to remain debt-free and economically responsible, as well. The Mormon approach is one of instilling social as well as religious values. The goal in mind is to create a happier, better educated, healthier, and more financially sound group of followers; and they seem to be achieving this goal in spades.

And while, given the subject matter, it would seem most prudent to zero in on the fundraising and educating prowess of this successful church organization, it is important that we not dwell on those matters as though they were the church's only noteworthy achievements. The fact is that the Church of Jesus Christ of Latter-day Saints not only manages to raise funds in order to better educate and instill values in its children, but that this act, in and of itself, truly *empowers* its followers as well. The educated and well-funded, after all, are far better equipped to live a comfortable life and pass on their values to the next generation. Given that notion, this empowerment approach seems to be exactly the kind of angle that Black and Hispanic churches in America would do well to adopt. For the Mormons, a large part of the congregant base is happy, psychologically and economically healthy, well-educated, and carries a truly steadfast vision of the future, even with its large minority base. In other words, the average member of the LDS Church wields the kind of personal power it takes to get ahead and stay ahead in life.

Suggesting that Black churches model their initiatives after those of the Mormon faith obviously has the potential to raise some red flags among the staunchest Baptist, Methodist, or Pentecostal followers among us. In response to this common misconception, I would like to point out that I in no way advocate the concept of more closely aligning ourselves with the *religious* beliefs of the Mormon Church. I merely suggest that we examine their triumphs in the realms of education and fiscal empowerment.

Another common objection to this proposal is that the Mormon Church is obviously so successful because they are largely White and privileged. First of all, this most frequent prejudice seems to be based entirely on misunderstanding. Many seem to think that all Mormons live in Utah where the congregant base (in fact, the entire population) is, indeed, mostly White. To say that all Mormons live in Utah, however, is a gross underestimation of the scope of this vast church. Would it surprise you to learn that the Church of Jesus Christ of Latter-day Saints is comprised of more than 12.5 million members worldwide? It should also be pointed out that the sheer geography of this organization and its members spans 160 nations. In fact, when global membership is taken into account, White people are actually the *minority* within the LDS Church—with over 55% of Mormons being non-White.

Furthermore, even if this most common misconception *were* true, I would like to suggest that there is a great deal more to rising above educational and economic setbacks than the color of one's skin or the money that one has at his disposal. There is a reason, after all, why the followers of this religion tend to fall so consistently among the middle- and upper-class population of America while other White churches cannot live up to the same standards of monetary success. As we will see later in this chapter, as well, it isn't enough to say that race plays the most significant role in financial gain on the part of a church body. There are many Black religious associations that have a great deal of money at hand.

To demonstrate the discrepancy in the social values displayed by these two significant church institutions (and, once again, I am lumping all Black churches, regardless of sectarian following, into one category), I offer the following section.

The Education

I will begin with a brief outline of two of the more unique central goals that the Mormon Church, as an institution, publicly represents. In short, Mormon leaders have historically and visibly mandated that their followers attempt to place their children in a position of power by keeping their own financial matters in order. In addition, this church freely recognizes the importance of an educated following. As such, they command a greater understanding of what it takes to gain a proper education and a more unified and better structured methodology to achieving that end. In perpetuating the values of financial independence and higher education, the church has thereby ensured its future as a successful organization.

With its Church Educational System (CES), the largest body of the Mormon Church, the Church of Jesus Christ of Latter-day Saints, educates somewhere in the neighborhood of 1.2 million students and adult learners. By institutionalizing their own school programs, they have managed to proactively secure a brighter future for a massive cross-section of their following.

The religious and the secular are combined to form one all-encompassing approach to Christian education in the two main branches of the CES (known as "Seminary" and

"Institute"). According to their national website (www.ld-sces.org), the mission of the CES, as a whole, "is to assist the individual, the family, and priesthood leaders in accomplishing the mission of the church by:

1. Teaching students the gospel of Jesus Christ as found in the standard works and the words of the prophets.
2. Teaching students by precept and example so they will be encouraged, assisted, and protected as they strive to live the gospel of Jesus Christ.
3. Providing a spiritual and social climate where students can associate together.
4. Preparing young people for effective Church service.

While the subject matter may not be agreeable to the non-Mormon Christian, the methodology, at the very least, should be broadly considered. The true crux of the LDS CES approach is the third point on the list. To provide a *spiritual* and *social* climate in which students can feel comfortable associating with one another is the single greatest method to ensure that they are getting the positive interactive support that they need from one another and from responsible adults.

Through their Seminary and Institute programs, the LDS Church does just that. Both, at their cores, are essentially after-school programs. The first concentrates on shaping young people toward the ultimate path in the Mormon Church; to gain the kind of religious and secular education it takes to serve a mission and eventually attend college.

According to the CES website, "The seminary program offers weekday religious instruction for youth who attend public, private, or home schools." The Seminary is only for those students who are entering high school or who are at least 14 years of age before the coming school year begins.

The Institute program, on the other hand, essentially carries the torch once Seminary has been completed. Offering a kind of safe haven from the storms of everyday life, Institutes of Religion house a fun and engaging environment for young, single people between the ages of 18 and 30. As a series of physical buildings dotting the landscape of the multinational Mormon Church, they are "concerned with education for eternity and [provide] an opportunity for students to be touched and nurtured by the Spirit. Regular weekday classes are conducted on a variety of religious subjects, and students are provided an opportunity to associate spiritually, socially, and culturally with others of similar ideals."

These two distinct programs aren't exactly under-supported, either. They are headed by several governing bodies, including the Church Board of Education and Board of Trustees, the Office of the Church Commissioner or Education, and the Presidents of the various Mormon Institutes of Higher Education. In addition, regular attendees and graduates of these programs are encouraged to attend one of four largely Mormon colleges in the U.S. (BYU, BYU Hawaii, BYU Idaho, and LDS Business College).

One of the most intriguing aspects of the CES program is that the education is not centered entirely upon the classroom.

Both seminary and secular values are taught in before and after school programs typically held at Mormon-sponsored or owned meetinghouses (often located near public schools) or conducted privately at home. The curriculum for such courses of study is openly and regularly shared during worship services.

The Money

The most captivating (and perhaps controversial) aspect of the backdrop of the Mormon faith is its vast amounts of wealth and prodigious pursuit of monetary gain. In an article entitled "Kingdom Come: Salt Lake City was Just for Starters" (*Time Magazine*, August 4, 1997), author David Van Biema points out that this success has not come on the back of luck or social standing, either. In fact, it can be argued that the followers of the Church of Jesus Christ of Latter-day Saints, as what was once considered a wildly heretical faith, faced persecution similar to that of the many minority or religious subgroups in America throughout the 100 year period that began in the middle 1800s.

But today, in rising above their historical (and remarkable) social displacement, the Mormons have managed to construct themselves one of the wealthiest religious-based empires in the world. As Van Biema suggests, "There is no major church in the U.S. as active as the Latter-day Saints in economic life, nor, per capita, as successful at it." In fact, they have met with so much success that, "Stephen R. Covey bottled parts of the ethos in *The Seven Habits of Highly Effective People*...[and] The FBA and CIA, drawn by a seemingly incorruptible rectitude, have instituted Mormon-recruitment plans."

While estimates of the wealth surrounding the vast amounts of Mormon holdings range anywhere from $5 billion to $30 billion, the point is not necessarily about how much they have earned but *how* they have earned it and *what they are doing with it.* Of course, they do owe a great deal of their financially-centric approach to the fact that, "Of some 112 revelations received by the first Prophet and President of the church, Joseph Smith, 88 explicitly address fiscal matters." They also have the benefit of a following that

Allowing members of the communities to lead church services opens the floor to a broader scope of religious opinion and thinking.

strictly adheres to the call to pay yearly tithes (or 10% of each congregant's annual earnings, from familial patriarchs on down to their youngest children). Giving 10%, of course, is not an uncommon decree, it is a figure derived directly from the Christian Bible, after all. It is what the LDS church *does* with their 10% that has made it so successful.

Rather than invest all of their profits in paying staff salaries and maintaining church buildings, the Mormons maintain a practice of allowing any and every member of the community to lead church services. This not only opens the floor to a broader scope of religious opinion and thinking, it introduces a great deal more secular debate (such as the conditions of local schools and the performance of member schoolchildren, for example) into the consciousness of its followers. In addition, it cuts out what would be a large part of the expenses for a massive and fast-growing church body. What remains of their earnings after maintenance has been addressed is reinvested into the many corporate holdings that the organization has managed to amass. Among these holdings is the 312,000 acre Deseret Ranch outside Orlando, Florida, America's largest producer of nuts, AgReserves, Inc.; Bonneville International Corp, an extraordinarily large radio chain; and the Beneficial Life Insurance Company. Investing in companies like these allows the faith to not only generate enormous amounts of wealth from what would otherwise be a donation pool fairly comparable to, say, the Catholic Church, but to keep the majority of the money in-house as well.

Through the Looking Glass

It is through the efforts listed above that the Mormon Church has managed to build such an enviable school system and effective approach to empowerment. And the truly discouraging aspect of all of this is that all it would take for the average

Black church to find similar success would be to begin with a very minor philosophical change. Rather than giving money and then complaining about where it is going, Black and other minority congregants simply need to do a better job of turning the struggle inward. As Van Biema puts it, "it is hard to argue with Mormon uniformity when a group takes care of its own so well. The church teaches that in hard times, a person's first duty is to solve his or her own problems and then ask for help from the extended family." In other words, the root of all potential problems, to the Mormon, is the person who is having the problem. That person, therefore, is primarily responsible for overcoming the issue him/herself. A Mormon's approach to a dilemma is to aggressively take matters into his/her own hands.

> The first roadblock is, "We don't have enough money."...The second is usually generated by the size of a congregation.

Conversely, a large cross-section of low-income minority churchgoers seems too ready to blame others for their own misgivings. Conversations regarding finance and education do not happen readily enough within the walls of minority churches. Perhaps we are not discussing things to the degree that we should because so many of the followers of our churches are struggling to make ends meet, greatly hindering any would-be dialogue on financial independence. While this condition is certainly the core of the problem, it is not the only deciding factor on why Black churches remain so handcuffed when it comes to properly amassing wealth and using it to exact real social change.

At many minority churches, for example, the only financial issue that the congregants seem to want to discuss is how much of their donation money the Pastor is spending on himself. Traditionally, we seem to get more hung up on what our church leaders are driving to work than what the Bible says we are obligated to give. Rather than fight the good fights, like demanding funds for the building of a local outreach program or sewing seeds into a scholarship fund for the children that attend our churches, we silently and privately complain about how our donations have been misappropriated.

While the leaders of the LDS church, over the course of 150 years, have managed to construct a wealth-generating religious machine that, through both doctrine and social practice, keeps its eye squarely on the future, the average low-income minority church seems to remain a bit too reactionary. We focus a little too much on the here and now. Before and after worship services, there appears to be more discussion about how we look (our clothes, our hair, our nails; mainly things that depreciate and have no lasting value at all) than about what we need to do to better our children's future. And the needed shift in focus is so simple. What kind of difference would it make, for example, if even five women in every minority congregation realigned just one of their monthly installments for nail-appointments and donated that same $50 to a church-sponsored scholarship fund? If every Black or Brown churchgoer in America did as the Mormons do and skipped two meals per month in order to donate the resultant extra money to religious-based charities, how much more could we save for our church's (and our own) financial independence?

It's Not the Money

The first and most common reaction to the claim about the benefits of saving for the future is that, religiously and racially, comparing Black churches to Mormon churches is like comparing apples to oranges. Well, I have already dispelled the myth of the LDS Church being mostly White and religion, as far as this chapter is concerned, has absolutely nothing to do with the issue. Still, Mormon churches, my detractors would say, just have more money to invest. While this is true, LDS church holdings do absolutely and unequivocally dwarf those of comparable minority religious groups (and even most other White churches, for that matter), I posit that it is not the most important piece of the puzzle.

For an example of why I feel that one does not need to begin with wealth to amass wealth, and that I further stipulate that race has nothing to do with the ability to financially ensure a brighter future for oneself and one's children, look no further than the Potter's House near Dallas, Texas. According to its website (www.thepottershouse.org), this group is a "non-denominational church...that was founded in 1996. In just over seven years, The Potter's House grew from 50 families to more than 28,000 members who step out in force, inspired and spiritually armed by Bishop T.D. Jakes to help others in their communities and across the world. *Christian Today* and the *Dallas Morning News* tag The Potter's House church as one of the fastest growing churches in the nation."

The thing that truly separates The Potter's House church (which has a following that is 77% African-American, 13% White, 7% Hispanic and 3% other minorities) from other predominantly minority churches is not its remarkable rate of growth, however. Rather, it is its philosophical approach to financial stewardship. Not only are the group's congregants remarkably faithful to its religious teachings (many have to stand in line for hours just to get in on a Sunday service), they are much more active in church-sponsored programs than the average minority churchgoer, as well. It is not just the fact that they pay tithes and regularly give offerings, either. The leaders of The Potter's House have banded together with their vocal congregants to properly earmark funds to specific areas most in need of financial growth.

Through the efforts of his followers, Bishop T.D. Jakes has managed to generate enough funding to build an unmatched religious and social commemoration known as "MegaFest." This annual festival combines topics ranging from male and female empowerment to youth advancement to comedy, music and fashion. Not only does MegaFest represent an astonishingly thriving fundraiser, it is a celebration of what it means to be a proud minority citizen, and gives many great speakers and entertainers a forum for preaching the word of social as well as religious success. In addition to MegaFest, another clerical focus that may be of interest is that the church regularly honors its own students via events that mark both public and private school graduations. How rarely this kind of effort is duplicated in smaller, minority churches.

In truth, The Potter's House is not entirely unique, either. It is just one of an emerging new breed of Black "Mega-Churches" that have risen above the squabbling of what it takes to get ahead and banded together to form

It is not the size of these powerhouse associates that makes the difference. It is *how* they choose to raise and spend their money...that has brought them such incredible success.

a religious base for generating true and measurable social change. But I do not intend to suggest that the Mega-Church route is the only path to success. Of course, I realize that not every religious institution can be a Mega-Church and that not all minority-based churches can or should aspire to become one. It is not the size of these powerhouse associations that makes the difference. It is *how* they choose to raise and spend their money. It is the proactive, rather than reactive stance, that has brought them such incredible and rapid success.

The Outlook and How to Shift It

Most Black and other minority churches do not do all that they can to prepare their youth for becoming financially and educationally empowered. As a result, many of these same churches have fallen into such poverty that they seem to feel there is no answer. Conversely, we find many predominantly Black institutions that have managed to traverse the waters of racial oppression to achieve a small-scale version of the kind of success enjoyed by their Mormon counterparts. The LDS church and Mega-Churches are on the rise not because of their access to wealth or because of the color of their skin, but because of their outlook and concentration on a centralized and highly-publicized set of financial, educational and social goals.

The final most common objection to the prospect of promoting educational outreach programs (and funding for such programs) is a matter of simple size.

In closing, I would like to provide an anecdote that should prove that it is not the size, race, or monetary backing of a religious institution that truly matters. In Sacramento, California, we find a house of worship known as the St. Paul Missionary Baptist Church (www.stpaulsac.org). Its leader, Dr. (and Pastor) Ephraim Williams managed to mold a small, struggling church into a force to be reckoned with in the Sacramento area. Serving almost as the backbone to this kind of achievement was the Pastor's insistence upon the importance of paying off the mortgage to the church building in short order. He publicly and repeatedly emphasized that ownership is the key to financial empowerment and that, as such, the vast majority of the funds donated to the church would go towards meeting that end. In addition, once the building was paid off, he vowed to build a new Life Center on the land adjacent to the church, where volunteers could help teach local children about life issues such as avoiding drugs and performing well in school. It would be a place where entrapped children could come to play basketball, receive tutoring, or participate in other kid-centric (and sometimes child-led) activities.

Of course, Pastor Williams found that his congregants, given that they knew exactly where their money was going, gave much more willingly and generously than most. He saw his goal of paying off the church mortgage come to fruition in less than 10 years. Today, the Life Center that had quickly become the central goal of the entire church is in existence and making a huge difference in many local Sacramento communities.

Meanwhile, there remain scores of minority churches in southern California (and elsewhere), that get by on middling social success at best. This deluge of poor, predominantly

Black or Brown churches (indeed, there seems to be one on every corner in many impoverished neighborhoods), never seems to get to a level of being able to command any kind of power in the communities that they represent. These churches are typically small and see very little (if any) expansion over the course of many decades. I posit that this is not necessarily because their congregants are not generous. In fact, I would state just the opposite; poor people who are still willing to give to their churches are perhaps the most generous people in the country. It is just that too many of these same institutions, with their faithful and generous followings, are failing to have the kind of discussions that are so dire when it comes to bettering oneself. It is especially critical to open the floor to financial and educational dialogue when dealing with a congregation that is largely under-educated and impoverished in the first place. There is no training, there is only preaching. And for whatever reason (misunderstanding, misplaced blame, apathy, tacit approval), over the course of 50 years of what should have been empowerment following the Civil Rights era, the conversation remains largely the same.

CHAPTER 7

Beyond the Roadblocks:
Educating the Youth,
Regardless of Congregant Numbers
or Church Financing

I have spent the majority of the pages in this book suggesting that churches of color are failing to live up to their tremendous potential to exact real change in the struggling communities that surround them. With this chapter, I intend to demonstrate that, in several cases, that simply is not true. While the fact remains that we lack a unified, nationalized, proactive approach as a larger body of Black and Hispanic churches, this does not mean that one cannot find the proverbial diamonds scattered throughout the rough.

Indeed, if one were to search the archives of newspapers or the sprawling space of information that is the Internet, one would have no trouble uncovering random success stories from minority churches all across America. The three church groups that I intend to present in the pages that follow certainly fall within that category. The unfortunate fact, however, is that they represent a relatively minor sample size when one considers the sheer numbers of like organizations in this country.

The idea seems simple. For one, we have a religious body that is committed to the improvement of its people via faith and trust in the Lord. For another, we have a surrounding community in deep crisis concerning the path and tendencies of its young people. The solution should be obvious. The God-fearing, charitable organization should jump at the opportunity to help those most in need (and, indeed, those closest to its doorstep). The problem is that, when faced with the prospect of promoting and developing significant outreach programs, many churches falter and stumble over the same roadblocks.

The first roadblock is, "We don't have enough money." As we will see from the Churches Supporting Churches (CSC) affiliated churches in New Orleans, the amount of cash in a dowry could not be further from the realm of relevance. For the innovator in America, there is *never* a shortage of funding. Church organizations like the CSC managed to raise considerable sums of money despite being in one of the most impoverished regions of the country and having a population that was both geographically and spiritually displaced by the worst natural disaster in this country's history.

The second roadblock is usually generated by the size of a congregation. Without the numbers of religious organizations like Mount Zion, most churches feel somehow humbled to the point of palpable inactivity and, concurrently, a sense of tacit passivity. The whole "let someone else do it," mentality, unfortunately, is exactly what causes the kind of conditions that prompted me to sit down and write this book in the first place. If "let someone else do it," were an acceptable ideology, *everyone's* children would be performing poorly in school. The point, then, is not the size of the church. The point is the *willingness* to make a difference. Remember the old cliché: It only takes one mind to save a child. Thus, even in a congregation of only 50 adults, there exists the potential to save at least 50 children.

For now, I do not intend to offer specific direction on how to achieve the kind of value that I promote in this book; for the moment, think of these shining examples of charitable work as a roadmap of sorts. These three churches of varying size (coupled with the many charitable organizations listed in Chapter 8) should help to illustrate the pure geography of the situation. Later, I will build upon that landscape by adding a comprehensive set of how-to instructions to the picture.

The Moneymakers

The title of "moneymaker," in this case, goes to a church that admittedly is quite large. In fact, it is the "oldest and largest historically African American Baptist Church in the State of Washington," (www.mountzion.net). The intriguing thing about Mount Zion Baptist Church, however, is not its size or even that it has managed to raise a great deal of money; it is how prolifically they have done it. No Baptist church in the entire country raises more money for student scholarships than Mount Zion. And I suggest that they have done this not because of their size, but rather, because of their outlook on the responsibility of a church to its own community: "Mount Zion Baptist Church is a growing, thriving church dedicated to building a vibrant Christian community built on principals that embrace social justice as central to our mission...We believe that we are called to be a Christ-centered church that addresses the needs of the total person through liberating worship, life-transforming Christian education, progressive and timely ministries focused on effective social activism."

Mount Zion serves its surrounding community with an unprecedented 40 specialized ministries. Each ministry is headed by a different leader or group of leaders (who meet regularly to discuss the direction of their own program). Of the 40 ministries that Mount Zion supports, there are a few low-dollar options and a few that are a little costlier. For the cost-conscious church, consider the following:

"Advisory Council": This is essentially a group that gets together weekly to discuss the most pressing needs of the church and the surrounding community. These individuals should take it upon themselves to do the research and leg-work necessary to determine the areas that should be of greatest concern to the congregation and its ministers. When the time comes (every Sunday or every other Sunday, perhaps), it is the obligation of this council to present their findings to the other members of the church. At Mount Zion, the pastor serves as moderator, to keep the meetings in order. All attendance at these discussions and brainstorming sessions is optional, of course, but I think that one would be surprised at the interest that this would draw from most congregants.

"Boys to Men": Mount Zion promotes this aptly named program as an avenue for more experienced, responsible male adults to mentor the younger males in the community and church. The "ministry was designed to help boys to become men through teaching vision, values, and virtue. The goals…are to teach academic growth, personal growth, interpersonal growth, business, and workplace knowledge." This may be a more cost-effective program since it runs entirely upon volunteer efforts on the part of the men in the community.

Among the ministries that may require a little more funding, consider the holistic approach that Mount Zion takes to "Christian Education." In combining their morality with their own take on educational advancement, this program works to keep children away from the temptations of modern life and in the classrooms; all with a good, Christian value structure to serve as the guiding light. Essentially, the entire program is run by a dozen elected leaders who "organize, administer, and supervise the entire educational programs of the church." While most churches are not capable of electing a body of twelve members, the concept can be simplified: a group of people, however large or small, should be elected by the congregation to spearhead the educational outreach effort. The minister, in other words, with all his/her existing obligations, cannot be expected to do it alone. Initiatives falling within the "Church School" program include everything ranging from vacation bible retreats to adult education. The most noteworthy (and probably cost-effective) arm of the Church School system is known as the "Educational Excellence Program." It calls for the direct recognition (during and after church services) of academic achievement on the part of school-age congregants. "Students who submit report cards are given certificates of appreciation, savings bonds, calculators, bicycles, and other gifts." While many churches would not be able to afford giving such lavish gifts, the benefit of simple recognition remains the same.

The final educational outreach concept is what makes Mount Zion so noteworthy. Annually, it raises more money for scholarships than almost any religious organization in the country. Scholarships range from $500 to four years of full tuition at a college or university. The truly intriguing aspect of this achievement, however, is that Mount Zion is not able to do this because it has an extremely wealthy congregation. It manages to raise so much money through sheer ingenuity. Among the fundraisers are a request for memorial grants and scholarships, an annual auction, corporate and individual donations (both in person and online), community gatherings and ticketed events (luncheons, children's festivals, speeches from public figures like Sen. Barack Obama, annual retreats, etc.), and an online store (where they sell books, CDs and videos from Baptist artists).

The Survivors

Hurricane Katrina brought with it arguably the most devastating disaster in this country's history. Many of the horrors that came out of New Orleans during the aftermath will be indelibly etched into the minds of generations. Despite all of this, however, there are thousands of stories of triumph owed to the inherently steadfast resolve of mankind.

One such success story comes in the form of two Black church leaders who took it upon themselves, in spite of the poverty of the region and the extraordinary lack of physical re-sources to draw from, to make a difference in the lives of those who most need help. In a region of the world that could have seen many of its historic minority churches close its doors for-ever, these two men saw to it that not only did the parishes not die out, their charitable programs remained operational as well. Their story holds two lessons: 1) There is no such thing as not enough money and 2) In the absence of true resources, it is sometimes better to band together in order to meet a need.

According to an article by Jane Lampman entitled, "To Raise New Orleans, Life Churches, Pastors Urge" (*Christian Science Monitor*, August 24, 2006), Reverend C.T. Vivian of Atlanta partnered with Reverend Dwight Webster of New Orleans to form "Churches Supporting Churches (CSC), a national initiative to revitalize 36 churches in the 12 hardest-hit areas." The central goal of the CSC is to connect each struggling New Orleans church with the charitable donations and support of at least 10 Black churches in other parts of the country. Through these efforts, not only can the group help to re-open the doors of many Louisiana congregations, they can hope to keep their community outreach programs up and running as well, and, in New Orleans, this is obvi-ously an area of deep concern.

The lesson to take from this story is that sometimes it is better for those churches who are too small or in need of monetary aid to band together financially with those groups that are in the best position to help. The power of the many far outweighs the power of the few.

It's All Relative

The final most common objection to the prospect of promoting educational outreach programs (and funding for such programs) is a matter of simple size. Many congregants in rural towns or small churches seem to believe that they cannot hope to make a difference because they do not have the numbers to do so. The concept is simple: educational programs cost money, and the fewer the people, the smaller the pool of potential resources.

The only trouble with this argument is that there are literally thousands of churches in this country that refuse to follow this stereotype. Each has managed to fly in the face of the odds by raising large sums of money and conducting highly beneficial educational curriculum for their student-age congregants. In the hopes of demonstrating that this occurrence could be the norm rather than an aberration, this section outlines the efforts of three different churches from three different towns, and representing three different races/religions.

As author Kirk Noonan so eloquently puts it in his article entitled "A Leap of Faith in Tiny Timbo" (*Today's Pentecostal Evangel Magazine*, October 2004), the Timbo Valley Assembly of God in Timbo, Arkansas, "sits on a hilltop glistening like a crown jewel perfectly out of place in such a rural area…Though seemingly out of place, the church is a symbol of what God can do when a tiny congregation takes a giant leap of faith.

"'When we started building this church there were two schools of thought,' admits Senior Pastor Dave Campbell...'Some people said I had heard from God; others said I was crazy.'

"Crazy because Timbo is in Stone County, where the average income hovers around $20,000 per year. Crazy because the congregation was small. Crazy because the church had never undertaken such a project."

In short, the Timbo Valley Assembly of God began with a dowry of $400 and a congregation of only 30 people. In the hopes of raising money for a new church and the support of a series of missions and other outreach programs, Campbell began by requesting that, collectively, the church give $100 per month to the church's charitable concerns. What he found was that, given an objective, his congregation was willing to meet the request and then some. By year's end, the church was raising $400 per month. Today, they are one of the most charitable small town churches in America, having donated over $50,000 to missions in a five-year period.

Another small town church, Old Elam Missionary Baptist Church in Hearne, Texas, has seen a great deal of success in the avenue of youth education. As one of the oldest Black churches in Texas, Old Elam has been preaching its message since 1863. Today, despite what might be considered a slight size when compared to some of the churches found in large cities, Old Elam offers a wide range of extra-curricular activities designed to help the youth within its walls gain a better understanding of religious and secular education. Children at this enterprising church are welcome to engage in youth outreach programs, the choir, drill and praise teams, mime groups and bible lessons. All programs are designed to help the child become a more well-rounded member of society and faithful follower of God.

St. Jude Church in Glennvill, Georgia, meanwhile, is a primarily Hispanic church that understands and promotes the educational approach to the betterment of society as well. Despite the fact that they have very few congregants and a smaller range of financial resources, they offer regular public education programs in addition to their bible studies, prayer and worship sessions and fellowship programs. They are staunch proponents of the service agenda and believe a very large portion of that agenda, for Latin Americans, is to improve performance in school. What's more, they believe that change is better handled by a coalition rather than an individual. Their "Building Interchurch Relationships" program seeks to connect the churches of similar values in the state of Georgia.

Regardless of geographical location or socio-economic conditions, a motivated church can (and does) make a difference in the lives of many struggling students.

Regardless of geographical location or socioeconomic conditions, a motivated church can (and does) make a difference in the lives of many struggling students. The money for the kind of programs that this book intends to advocate can be had as long as a congregant base is willing to work for it. Whether you are in Dixon, Illinois; Wheaton, Missouri; or Bethany, Virginia; your church holds the power to exact real change.

Conclusion

In the following chapter, you will find a summary of a small cross-section of charitable organizations not affiliated with churches that are doing their part to make a difference in the lives of our children. While these groups are certainly making a noble effort, the fact remains that their work is, for the most part, hindered by sheer geography. There are those who make a difference in New York. There are those who make a difference in Sacramento. There are those who make a difference in New Orleans. Imagine, for a moment, if every church on every corner of every city in America followed a concrete plan to get our kids off the streets and into the classroom. As a unit, the Black and Hispanic Church in America is tantamount to a slumbering giant. If even half of them were to follow in the footsteps of Vivian and Webster, and band together to form extra-curricular charitable foundations that do not dally with religious value systems, we would be left with a fully functioning educational revolution.

PART THREE

The Solution

If service is the rent you pay for your existence on earth, are
you behind in your rent?

—*Robert G. Allen*

CHAPTER 8

A Common Cause:
What Other Minority Organizations Are
Doing to Help Solve the Problem

Of course, this book would be remiss if, in the absence of a truly uniform activist stance on the part of the church, it failed to highlight what some of the other minority organizations are doing to help children of color. As such, an illustration of the true and demonstrable success of several non-religious organizations is in order. After all, as discussed in the previous chapter, without a cohesive front of ideas to help us all move forward, we will remain engulfed in our middling and disorganized educational charity efforts as a religious body.

What is more, in examining the goals of these organizations, we can come to adopt them as our own. On the surface, this chapter offers the first glimpse into what we as a church could and should be doing to help our children succeed. But perhaps there is more than just that. Perhaps it is not beyond the realm of imagination to assume that alliances between minority churches and these charitable organizations are both possible and natural. Such a union would benefit both parties, after all, as volunteer numbers and the pool of charitable donations and funding would be greatly expanded.

Our roadmap isn't truly complete until we have established what the end of the road looks like; until we have determined exactly what the goal needs to be. The following organizations have already taken strides to move away from traditional passivity when it comes to the education of Black and Hispanic children. And it is my belief that we would all do well to model our efforts after theirs.

Of the many Black and Hispanic organizations that have made an honorable difference in the lives of thousands of minority children, not least among them are the fraternity and sorority programs known as "the Great Eight." At the risk of sounding like Greek alphabet soup, I dare to list them here: Alpha Phi Alpha, Alpha Kappa Alpha, Omega Psi Phi, Delta Sigma Theta, Kappa Alpha Psi, Sigma Gamma Rho, Phi Beta Sigma and Zeta Phi Beta. Of the lot of them, my analysis will admittedly be most biased toward the fourth on the list, Delta Sigma Theta, since I am an active and financial member of that organization. For the sake of avoiding redundancy, I will provide an in-depth look at only the first four. This is not to say that the latter four are lesser organizations; indeed, I would suggest that they all operate on and succeed within a level playing field as far as charitable work is concerned.

Moving away from traditionally collegiate programs, it is clear that there are many other groups that incite positive change outside the walls of the church (although it is important to note that many do depend on churches to help house and facilitate their programs). Among them is, of course, the NAACP. This historic and revered organization has arguably made the greatest impact of any minority-focused program in the history of this country. In addition, we find the Urban League, the 100 Black Men/Women Association, Jack and Jill, The National Alliance of Black School Educators and any number of other innovative groups. Turning to the Hispanic front, we find no shortage of charitable organizations, either. MANA, the League of United Latin American Citizens and the Congressional Hispanic Caucus Institute are just three of the hundreds of groups dedicated to improving the education and lifestyle of this critical American demographic.

My hope is that a quick look at this admittedly small cross-section of minority charitable associations will help church leaders realize that there is so much more we can do to take a stand on our children's future. At the very least, perhaps this chapter will spark some new lines of thinking within the walls of your own church, big or small. Whatever the case, it is important that those among us best in position to exact real change take it upon themselves to work to develop programs similar to those listed below. Each has its own tremendous value. Each has at least a chance to pull thousands of lives away from the brink of social and educational disaster.

Alpha Phi Alpha

The first of our charitable Black fraternities is celebrating its 100th year of existence this year. According to their national website (www.alphaphialpha.net), since their inception in 1906, the group has "supplied a voice and vision to the struggle of African Americans and people of color around the world." It was the first intercollegiate Black fraternity in America and it was established at Cornell University in Ithaca, New York.

"The Fraternity initially served as a study and support group for minority students who faced racial prejudice, both educationally and socially, at Cornell." Today, this enterprising organization has led to the development of Alpha University, an agenda that works to promote brotherhood, leadership training and educational outreach. Centering on the concept of mentoring, the leaders and participants within the fraternity have developed three key programs that cater to the advancement of young Black males. The first of the trio is known as "Go-to-High-School, Go-to-College"— an initiative that pairs Alpha men with groups of young people in an effort to reinforce the importance of "completing secondary and collegiate education as a road to advancement." "Project Alpha," another of the three main programs, "is designed to provide education, motivation, and skill-building on issues of responsibility, relationships, teen pregnancy, and sexually transmitted diseases for young males, ages 12 to 15 years." The final curriculum, "A Voteless People is a Hopeless People," is an agenda that promotes the importance of voting through town meetings and candidate forums.

Alpha Kappa Alpha

Our second charitable collegiate organization followed closely on the heels of Alpha Phi Alpha in its inception. Founded in 1908, Alpha Kappa Alpha represents the oldest Black sorority in the U.S. Through their central outreach initiative known as "The Heart of ESP: An Extraordinary Service Program," they have set up a platform of service that is five-fold, or, as they say on their official website (www.aka1908.com), it is a program that "responds to the contemporary needs of the Black community with comprehensive non-traditional programs."

The first of these five platforms is known as "Non-Traditional Entrepreneur," an effort that works to empower prospective minority small business owners with a track to achievement via networking and mentoring programs. The second is called "Economic Keys to Success." "Through education, synergy, and partnerships," it works to improve standards of living within Black communities. The third, "Economic Growth of the Black Family," allies itself closest to the premise of this book. As the Black church is the central focus of the betterment of youth and community, this platform understands that the family unit plays an even bigger role. It toils to improve the foundation of familial relationships and even plays a part in supporting young Black males in their efforts to overcome the many formidable temptations that they face everyday.

Omega Psi Phi

Founded in 1911 at Howard University, Omega Psi Phi has enjoyed a long and proud history of academic and communal service. Their programs are many, so it may be most appropriate to simply summarize all those that align themselves the closest to the agenda of this book.

According to its national website (www.oppf.org), The Scholarship Program offers aid to Black undergraduate students (both members and non-members) via the contributions of its graduate-level participants. In addition, the group promotes an initiative known as "Social Action Programs," requiring all fraternity members to "facilitate, participate, and coordinate activities that will uplift their communities." Some of the activities listed as beneficial are voter registration, literacy training, Habitat for Humanity and other volunteer work, mentoring and fundraising. The group also focuses on health and education programs similar to those listed above. Other projects and requirements of note include a goal that centers on locating and encouraging (via financial and tutoring assistance) young people who are interested and talented in the arena of performing, arts and a mandate that all members of the various chapters of the fraternity remain active in the NAACP.

Delta Sigma Theta

Following in the footsteps of Omega Psi Phi, the Delta Sigma Theta sorority was founded at Howard University two years later on January 13, 1913. Today, "Delta Sigma Theta Sorority is a private, non-profit organization whose purpose is to provide services and programs to promote human welfare" (www.deltasigmatheta.org).

Their Five-Point Programmatic Thrust keys in on, obviously, five points of major concern for the African-American community. They are: Economic Development, Educational Development, International Awareness and Involvement, Physical and Mental Health, and Political Awareness and Involvement.

Concentrating on the Educational Development agenda, if I may be allowed a moment of shameless self-promotion, here, the Sacramento chapter of Delta Sigma Theta (the chapter that I am a part of; http://www.dstsacramentoalumnae.com) has issued two key components to this national curriculum. We have established the Dr. Betty Shabazz Jr. Academy, which "seeks to encourage and support the pursuit of educational achievement of African-American youth in the Sacramento community." Our modest student body of girls ages 9 to 15 attended the academy to better themselves in the areas of science, math and technology. The second major outreach program is known as Delta GEMS. Through this establishment, "Twenty members of our chapter currently participate in mentoring teenage girls." In partnering with San Juan Unified School District, the Fostering Hope Organization and the Coalition of 100 Black Women, we have implemented a mentoring program that focuses on career development, health and cultural awareness issues and literacy activities.

Fundraisers for such programs are spearheaded by our Ebony Fashion Show—a local event that sells more than 800 tickets annually. Ebony is our chapter's largest fundraiser to help support youth entering college. Scholarships range from $500 to full four-year awards that are given to the most deserving students.

Kappa Alpha Psi, Sigma Gamma Rho, Phi Beta Sigma, Zeta Phi Beta

The above listed fraternities and sororities are not without their public deeds, either. All of them host events and promote outreach programs similar to those covered above. The topic of note here is that each of these is a group that represents a concerned body of educated citizens and leaders, young and old, who have recognized a need to take action on the part of advancing children of color. Each and every one of these groups promotes a charitable educational agenda of some kind. For more information on these fraternities and sororities, look to the following official websites: www.kappaalphapsi1911.com, www.sgrho1922.org, www.pbs1914.org and www.zphib1920.org.

The Congressional Hispanic Caucus Institute (CHCI)

The CHCI now follows the creed that not only are Hispanics the largest minority population in the U.S., but they are the youngest, as well. As such, they arguably embody the greatest need for educational outreach. A population so heavily invested in its youth cannot fail its school-age generation, lest it face catastrophic social and economic conditions in the coming decades. At the same time, the group recognizes that the current Hispanic dropout rate, "is 2.5 times higher than that of African Americans and 3.5 times higher than the rate of non-Hispanic Whites," (www.chci.org). "CHCI is the only national Hispanic organization that offers a summer internship program, fellowship program, and scholarship awards for Hispanic youth." Essentially, their many programs focus on helping young people achieve that next step in life—for high school students, the goal is to reach college; for college students, it is getting a decent job; and so on. The importance of the parent in a child's educational and social life is not lost on this group, either.

Their programs are many. For more on the specific programs that this organization offers, see their website at www.chci.org. In summary, the site offers a list of disciplines on which they focus: High school education, higher education, parental involvement, workforce diversity, networking and coalition-building and leadership development.

NAACP

Of course, no discussion of minority activist groups would be complete without taking a look at the NAACP. While I have already covered a brief history of the organization, an outline of their various charitable efforts is certainly in order. Their many cultural advancement efforts are divided into ten key subgroups. They are: Youth & College; NAACP ACT-SO ("a year-long enrichment program designed to recruit, stimulate, improve, and encourage high academic cultural achievement among African-American high school students"); Women in the NAACP; the Washington Bureau; Development; Research, Advocacy and Training; the National Prison Project; Branch and Field Services; Legal; and Religious Affairs.

Of the many subgroups, the most relevant to our present study are Youth & College, NAACP ACT-SO, and Religious Affairs. The first was initiated in 1935 by Juanita E. Jackson. According to the NAACP website (www.naacp.org), the department was founded based on "the growing concerns of Black youth in America." Through its efforts, thousands of young people of color are empowered to make the right decisions in their teens and explore the possibility of attending college. This department also works to make funding available to those without the means to pursue higher education.

The second was founded in 1978 by author and journalist Vernon Jarret. It was developed in recognition of the fact that Black youth are so often pushed toward the influences of careers in entertainment or athletic achievement while spurning the avenues of "academic, artistic, and scientific prowess and expertise." This organization provides a forum for expression for all those young people who would demonstrate a desire to excel in these most critical disciplines by establishing competitions centered on the sciences, humanities and performing/visual arts.

And the final department, Religious Affairs, seeks to advocate the continued (and most valuable) strategic alliance between the NAACP and local church leaders. Ever since Dr. King, "The NAACP has always had a strong relationship with the religious community." Through its efforts, the Religious Affairs committee hopes to continue promoting the development and support of capable religious leaders throughout the country. It is their hope that, by educating pastors, ministers and congregants on the matters of the church's role in the continuing civil rights movement and the betterment of Black society, they can work to create a brighter future for communities of color.

MANA: A National Latina Organization

Founded in 1974, MANA is an organization that "empowers Latinas through leadership development, community service, and advocacy" (www.hermana.org). By building a national community of Hispanic women, this group hopes to heighten the quality of life for their people all across America.

The most significant program sponsored by this association is known as Hermanitas®. This "national initiative focused on encouraging adolescent girls to stay in school and pursue high academic goals" sees its agenda carried out through summer institutes, local workshops, a partnership with the Girl Scouts of America, an online mentoring program, community service efforts and initiatives that are based in primarily minority school districts.

"Hermanitas® empowers Latinas through education, leadership development, health and fitness, cultural awareness and community action. The program is designed to instill within future Latina leaders strong family and cultural values, integrity, self-esteem, self-awareness, pride and civic and cultural responsibility." To meet such an end, MANA chooses to concentrate its efforts on the three months out of the year that children are not in school. Through its National HERMANITAS® Summer Institute (NHSI), the organization educates approximately 140 elementary, middle and high school students from all corners of the country. "The NHSI program consists of the development of strategies that will raise awareness of the impact of their choices in life, and transform that understanding into action. This is accomplished through interactive workshops, reflections and inspirational journal writing, participation of Latina speakers of distinction in our communities, cultural and social activities, and resource information on all subjects addressed at the NHSI."

The Urban League

This well-run organization boasts many different charitable arms, none more important than its Education and Youth program, which is divided into six major subgroups. The National Achievers Society "recognizes, awards, and instills a sense of pride in students who excel academically" (www.nul.org). The Black Executive Exchange Program (BEEP) "enables corporate executives to give back, mentor, and teach college students." Another rather unique subgroup is known as the Hip Hop Reader, a New York City area program sponsored by Russell Simmons, Verizon, and New York City schools, which has installed a book club that promotes readership among teens by allowing them to trade "reading points" for merchandise.

The other three programs (GE/National Urban League Corporate Volunteer Program, National Urban League Incentives to Excel & Succeed and Read and Rise) advocate volunteerism, leadership skills and parental involvement in child literacy, respectively.

Jack and Jill

The mission statement of this assembly suggests that they aim to, "provide cultural, social, civic, and recreational activities that stimulate and expand the mind to enhance life." Founded in Philadelphia in 1938, this intrepid organization has spent the past seven decades bringing children of color together to learn and participate in group activities. The website (www.jack-and-jill.org) lists their goals as follows:

- To create a medium of contact for children, which will stimulate their growth and development.
- To provide constructive educational, cultural, civic, recreational, social, and service programs for children.
- To aid mothers in learning more about their children and childcare through educational conferences and workshops.
- To seek for all children the same advantages we desire for our own.
- To support all national legislation aimed at bettering conditions for all children.
- To develop and disseminate childcare and child development educational material.

League of United Latin American Citizens (LULAC)

Over the course of its more than 75 years of existence, LULAC has worked to exact many positive social and economic changes for Hispanics in America. Operating largely on the legal front, this organization has been responsible for landmark cases regarding civil rights, segregation, civic duties, voter rights and political participation. Their listed mission statement (www.lulac.org) says, "The Mission of the League of United Latin American Citizens is to advance the economic condition, educational attainment, political influence, health, and civil rights of the Hispanic population of the United States."

The group sets out to meet that end through many different charitable programs. Its policy summits, Legislative Gala, Women's Conference, National Convention and Federal Training Institute provide valuable forums for thousands of people on a yearly basis. The agenda for all of these conferences and initiatives is to promote the political, educational and occupational health and well-being of all Hispanic American citizens.

Its educational arm has three main extensions. The umbrella for the whole program is a network of building-fronts called LULAC National Educational Service Centers. Begun in 1973, the LNESC "centralized its educational effort in a network of sixteen counseling centers coordinated by an office in Washington, DC. LNESC's mission is to "increase educational opportunities for Hispanic Americans through the development and implementation of effective programs in Hispanic communities throughout the United States" (http://www.lulac.org/programs/centers.html). The second main initiative is a literacy program called "The Young Readers." Located at LULAC National Education Service Centers all across the country, this program "encourages children to make reading a life-long habit" (http://www.lulac.org/programs/literacy.html). And the third initiative is essentially a series of fundraisers designed to raise money for scholarships. "Since 1932 LULAC Councils have been selling tacos, tamales, having dances, etc., to raise monies for scholarships

that are given to Hispanic students meeting certain guidelines"
(http://www.lulac.org/programs/scholar.html).

The National Alliance of Black School Educators

Born of a dissertation examining Black-superintendent-led
school systems, this alliance was the brainchild of Dr. Charles
D. Moody Sr., who, together with several other African American school leaders, created a support network in the hopes of
enhancing the foundations of colored schools everywhere.

According to Dr. Moody, "When one is in a struggle or
battle, he looks around to see if he is alone. This human char-
acteristic was one of the underlying factors in the formation
of [this alliance]." A valuable lesson, to be certain. In any
case, this alliance has worked to set up annual conferences,
the National Education Policy Institute (NEPI), various public
forums, news briefs and commissions on how to improve
impoverished, underperforming and otherwise disadvantaged
school systems. Through the vision of one, a network of
minds was created—a network that has a greater capacity to
service the needs of the many.

The NABSE Annual Conference, "held every Novem-
ber…attracts nearly 4,000 conferees for four days of inspiring
plenary sessions, school tours, informative presentations and
educational workshops…[the] Conference is also the site of
the Annual Hall of Fame Awards, honoring outstanding

African Americans in the field of education and those who have made indelible contributions to the African American community" (http://www.nabse.org/about_programs.htm). Conferences such as this attract an attendee base that is almost 100% Black. Educators (from teachers to superintendents) representing minority and/or impoverished schools travel from all over the U.S. and Canada to be a part of this forum of new ideas and innovative educational approaches. Essentially, the session is intended to serve as a kind of symposium or "think tank" where theories and methods can be exchanged; but, even more than that, it is a place (a sanctuary of sorts) where educators can come annually to revive and rejuvenate themselves in preparation for another year of battling against the drifting tide of minority educational performance. To such an end, there are dozens of compelling lectures and breakout sessions offering insight into how other schools and districts have managed to get ahead of the curve. And a vendor network offers everything from books on the topic of minority education to the latest in software or other extracurricular programs to aid the cause.

Apart from conferences such as this, NABSE builds its mission and promotes its agenda through a series of public forums held all across the country and through "NABSE News Briefs"—a monthly newsletter available both online and in print.

Conclusion

If we can take example of the organizational skills of the Great Eight, the national focus of the NAACP and the centralized goals of programs like MANA or Jack and Jill, it is not difficult to imagine a nationalized agenda for the common good of Black and Hispanic church charitable programs emerging. In addition, because these organizations are so prevalent, odds are that the vast majority of minority churches in America have at least one member of at least one of these groups within its walls. Such valuable congregants could serve as the needed bridge to partnership with these intrepid groups. And if we can work to build alliances between our leaders—much as Dr. Moody once set out to do—we can further strengthen our role in the average community. As such, it is not a stretch to think that, as a church body, we can affect real change in the educational performance of children of color.

CHAPTER 9

Common Voice, Common Goal:
The Roadmap to Success
for the Church of Color

Numbers and reactions to those numbers, causes and effects, theories and stratagems—the pages of this book, to this point, have been littered with them. Given the clearly troubling circumstances surrounding the sliding educational performance of children of color, and the proposal that the church is in the best position to do more, a certifiable plan of attack is probably slightly overdue.

In numerous pockets of every city, there are hundreds (even thousands) of churches of color that are already doing a great deal to help their children.

Before unfolding the roadmap, it would be prudent to stress again that, in every corner of the country, in numerous pockets of every city, there are hundreds (even thousands) of churches of color that are already doing a great deal to help their children. In many minority churches, it is not uncommon to find a youth ministry that not only affects change within its own community, but one that employs many of the same concepts that this chapter attempts to outline, as well. This book is not an indictment of the churches that have already taken action; it is a call to arms for those that haven't.

Youth ministries are especially intriguing to this particular subject matter because they function much like a younger version of the church itself. Unless these well-intentioned programs are offered a cohesive plan from the adult contingent of the congregations that they serve, however, these otherwise righteous ministries may fall short of truly motivating our children to turn their backs on the streets and head to the library.

Another area for improvement across the board (even in those churches that have youth ministries and various other positive reinforcement programs in place) is the simple leadership structure that minority churches have so readily embraced. It seems that far too often, the burden of handling the everyday responsibilities of the church and its services, in addition to the tasks associated with sensible outreach initiatives, is left solely to the pastor, especially within a small congregation. The problem with this assumption is that it requires the Pastor to wear a few too many hats. Not only does he/she have to be a man/woman of God, he/she has to be well-read about local problems and in the know about all the background surrounding each of his/her congregants, both young and old. Plus, there is the sheer number of hours that must be committed to each of these varying tasks. Now, it would be foolish to suggest that there aren't pastors out there capable of doing all of this and more—but that's simply not the point. The point is that workloads like this would be taxing on anybody, even men and women of the utmost faith.

Perhaps the most troubling aspect of the entire picture we have before us, however, is that minority churches seem to hold the power to be one of the most charitable and beneficial non-profit organizations in an entire community.

People of every color and creed have always recognized the importance of giving in the name of their faith. Even in the poorest churches in the country, the collection plate very rarely goes empty. Chalk this up to the incredible will and generosity of our people.

Despite all of this, and because the sheer nature of the average minority church calls for leaving the church doors open to any and all charitable needs, not enough money is being earmarked to the benefit of our youth or the endowment of a yearly scholarship. The programs outlined in these pages will essentially change all of that without dipping into the funds already set up for other clerical needs; there is only so much potential for financial backing in even the smallest Black or Brown church, after all. Couple the methods within these pages with some of the more innovative fundraising approaches employed by many minority groups, both religious and non-religious, and we have the makings of a truly powerful network of funding and difference-making.

The remarkable thing about the youth education circumstances in which many minority communities find themselves entrenched is that they can be reversed fairly quickly. The secret is not to censure the students and tell them to try harder. The secret is to empower them and put them in position to work toward their own goals. Remember, children almost always tend to know what they want; they just may not yet know how to properly get it. Fortunately, through the strength of many of the following agendas, the proper path can surely be relayed.

A Public Education Leader

As alluded to already, our pastors are extremely busy. Even from the first Black or Brown church in America, we have realized that the task of leading a church is more than a full-time job. To expect the modern-day preacher to effectively lead a congregation, which is quite a feat in and of itself, maintain his/her own ecclesiastical studies, *and* spearhead the efforts of the many comprehensive outreach programs needed in the community, seems like a bit of a stretch. Certainly, there are many intrepid church leaders out there who fly in the face of this assertion, but the fact remains that not all of them are capable of taking on such a heavy workload. Some are too committed to the strictly pastoral side of the job. Others are too focused on helping the community to center enough attention on the needs of the congregation. Some aren't as young as they used to be.

Whatever the cause for aid, the point is that almost any job, regardless of the worker charged with its completion, could be done better with the help of another. If pastors had more time to dedicate to a church service, they would be even better than they already tend to be. In addition, with the help of another leader to head up the charitable arm of the church, the pastor would have even more time to spend with the dozens, hundreds, or even thousands of his/her congregants—and each member of the church would benefit from the opportunity to get to know their pastor even better than they already do.

Now, with those thoughts in mind, imagine how much more effective an educational outreach program would be if there was one person *specifically assigned* to manage it.

The first point of recommendation for this chapter is that each church of color needs to appoint a leader that has free reign to talk to and advise pastoral staff on the condition and direction of all church-sponsored outreach programs for youth. This person ideally is well-versed (or at least desires to be well-versed) in the arena of public education. The first requirement is that this person remains strictly focused on the public education improvement efforts on the part of the church. He/she must also be willing and able to go into the schools, gather information and report back to the church. It helps if he/she is well-read on current educational legislation and maintains a working knowledge of the performance of local schools and their students via report cards, test scores and behavioral records. He/she should be capable of addressing the needs of the children within the church's walls first and in the community that surrounds the church second. Essentially, this person is almost like a teacher working within the church.

This pastor-appointed and congregation-approved public education leader should be put in a position of authority to govern over the many daily tasks that face the vast majority of non-profit organizations (which is exactly how we should think of every ministry program that our churches support, large or small). For our purposes, the person in question would be in charge of directing whatever initiatives that the congregation voted to institute regarding improving local educational performance.

Even though leading the education initiative is an awfully trying job, the combination of sheer charitable will and a small stipend (at minimum) is usually more than enough to recruit a capable volunteer. If this concept is proposed to the church, in fact, you are likely to be amazed at the sheer number of people willing to lend a hand. What's more, in larger places of worship, the appointed educational director may both need and want to take volunteers to fill out a support group to help him/her run things. In such churches, where possible (and, depending on the need demonstrated by the church's students),—the role of Public Education Leader should be a fully paid position, as well.

The first argument to this proposal is that many churches already have this position in place. Hundreds of capable organizations already employ a volunteer director of a youth ministry of some kind and, even in those communities, many of the children continue to fall behind in school. This is a fundamental misunderstanding. Youth groups have their benefits (as we will see later in the chapter, in fact); it is just that one cannot expect a youth group leader to coordinate all of those excellent extra-curricular activities (in his/her free time, no less) and still have time to visit the schools and follow up with and educate the children. Youth ministries, at their core, are designed to be fun and engaging efforts to help the young members of the church become more well-rounded members of the community. As such, youth ministries, on their own, do not take enough heed of No Child Left Behind, high school exit exams, or the GPAs of the children in the congregation. Youth ministries, like the churches that sponsor them, simply do not boast a high enough Public Education IQ.

> Youth ministries, on their own, do not take enough heed of No Child Left Behind, high school exit exams, or the GPAs of the children in the congregation. Youth ministries, like the churches that sponsor them, simply do not boast a high enough Public Education IQ.

These tendencies, on their own, are not entirely wrong, of course. It is definitely important to maintain a sense of the social and the religious within the youth ministry. It's just that one of the most significant arms of such an outreach program seems to go largely ignored. Public education should be a regular and focused topic. In addition, the church as a whole needs to be apprised to the educational agenda of the youth group. In order to do that properly, the ministry and its most direct leader must have a more prevalent voice in the Sunday service—or, at the very least, one Sunday per month.

Furthermore, these programs and their leaders do not tend to be well enough connected to the schools that the children attend. The public education leader (or the pastor-appointed head of the educational committee) must be held responsible for going into local schools, speaking directly with our children about their education and compiling the information for delivery to the congregation.

In summary, think of a public education leader not as another youth minister, but rather as a mouthpiece for the consortium of youthful ideas that is ready to be shared with its adult counterpart. Through the leader's intrepid reporting and tireless legwork, the congregation will finally be able to gain access to the kind of knowledge it takes to both assess and fight the problem.

Report and Recognize

If we realize the need for a responsible leader of the educational outreach movement, we can shift toward the understanding that no capable organization finds success without first researching the problem that it intends to face. In other words, we must compile the information surrounding the negatives before we can hope to eliminate them.

Almost everybody knows the gossip in their own church, but it's the wrong kind of gossip. Both before and after Sunday services in churches of color, there tends to be a great deal of socialization. The church in the minority community, therefore (and perhaps more than anywhere else), has the potential to be a social center. As such, it does not seem unreasonable to suggest that we dedicate at least a portion of the social time that typically occurs before and after church to attending structured meetings regarding the educational performance of our congregation's children.

The best method to improving the report cards that our children bring home is to create a report card *of* our church's children.

The only way to conduct any kind of structured meeting, of course, is to have proper and accurate data at hand. The first responsibility of our church-appointed youth leader, therefore, is to collect and compile spreadsheet reports on all the students within the congregation. This spreadsheet would best serve the cause if it contained the grade level, teacher, administrator, behavioral records, grade reports and standardized test information of each child. The beauty of this kind of information is that it is easily updated and would be invaluable to the youth minister, pastor and congregation.

To put all of this another way, the best method to improving the report cards that our children bring home is to create a report card *of* our church's children. How can we hope to improve the performance of our own kids if we don't even know where *we* stand? When summing up the relative futility in this particular discipline, the trouble is not that minority churchgoers don't want to help their kids improve. It isn't even that they fail to recognize sliding educational performance as a problem. The trouble in many cases is that too large a contingent of a congregation's adults tends to lack a true handle on what the kids are doing. A detailed report—coupled with weekly, biweekly, or even monthly presentations on that report—is the solution. History has taught us, after all, that the more we know, the more we are empowered.

The youth ministries already in place in many of these churches are in the perfect position to create such reports, as well. There is no reason that part of the requirement for being in a youth group can't be to provide a monthly update concerning educational and behavioral performance. If a child wants to continue participating in the many enjoyable social, extracurricular, or religious activities sponsored by the church, he/she must first (and regularly) supply a report card to the appointed ministry director. This requirement may be met with objections at first—but not once it's realized that this offers the potential for some personal gain, as well (more on this subject later).

A Word About Money

It would be beneficial to clear up one common objection: Money. The prevailing viewpoint in many churches, especially those without significant resources or weekly rates of attendance, is that all of the recommendations within these pages will cost too much. To those doubters, let it be known that no matter if you have two people in your church or two thousand, so long as the fundraising efforts are as innovative as they are transparent, the proper sum of money can always be had.

Consider the fact that $10 per month equates to only $2.50 per Sunday.

Take, for example, a rural church of color with only 50 adult members. Also, assume that the majority of these congregants live near the poverty line. If, in addition to the typical offerings given during church service, a collection plate is passed to supply outreach programs or scholarship funds, any house of worship can easily find the resources it needs. Say the pastor recommends a $10 contribution on a monthly basis. This may be met with objections, at first, but consider the ramifications of such an offering. Also, consider the fact that $10 per month equates to only

$2.50 per Sunday. And finally, take a moment to ponder the notion that, considering the steadily climbing prices of a Super-sized Value Meal at McDonald's, a monthly contribution of this amount barely exceeds the cost of one Big Mac, large fry and a Coke. Poor or no, there are very few people in this country who cannot afford to skip one meal at the drive-thru—especially when the sacrifice has the potential to paint an infinitely brighter future for their children. And, for those people who truly do not have $10 to spare, those who have more than $10 should be encouraged to cover for those who do not.

Now, take that average monthly contribution of $10 and multiply it by 50 (the stated number of adult members of the church). That comes out to $500 for an outreach program to operate on each month. Or maybe it comes out to one more semester that a college-bound member of the congregation does not have to pay for books. Either way, $500 per month from a church so small is an astonishing contribution—and an easily attainable one, as well. Running the math a bit further, $500 per month rounds out to $6,000 per year.

Skeptics may suggest that a budget such as this one cannot possibly support the trips to Disney World or Xbox 360s that children these days may demand as reward for good grades and exemplary behavior. To those skeptics, it should be pointed out that the example offered above was drawn from a church of only 50 people. In such a church, statistically, there is likely to be little more than a handful of preteen and teenage children in attendance. For six to eight teenagers, $6,000 per year can fund any number of beneficial activities, scholarship funds, or rapport-building trips.

Incentives, Incentives, Incentives

Now that the money is at hand, the question then becomes, how do you use it to get a child to perform better in school? There are a number of ways, but the first is to offer the same thing that almost everyone wants: rewards and recognition.

Before getting into all of that, an anecdote is warranted—in the hopes of illustrating the point that incentives have the tendency to work wonders even in the most impoverished communities.

While on a mission trip to La Vega in the Dominican Republic, I was introduced to a gentleman originally from Oakland, California. For our purposes, this gentleman shall remain nameless.

In his new home country, it is not unusual to find an exorbitant amount of squalor and despair. The all-too-large lower class segment of the Dominican population is often confined to slum-like conditions in the seemingly endless barrios of cities large and small. This particular gentleman, out of work and without hope, found himself in similar circumstances. He hit his bottom when, living at the time in Northern California, he nearly died of a drug overdose.

Like many narcotics stories with happy endings, my new friend told me of how, once he had seen the bottom, the only place to turn was up. He found the church and began clawing his way back to the top. Soon after, he began searching for what God wanted him to do and where He wanted him to be. Eventually, he took a mission trip to the Dominican and immediately realized that he had found his calling. While he had no formal training in Spanish, and the idea of living out his days in a Spanish-speaking country seemed almost absurd at first, he could not shake the notion that serving the Dominican people was what God had intended for him to do. To this day, the barrio is still the place that he calls home. In his time there, my new friend has managed to start a non-Catholic Christian church and school in the heart of the barrio, where faith lies in the Catholic Church at a 94% rate.

But none of this explains why his story bears mentioning. In short, this gentleman bears mentioning not simply because he represents a success story, but because of what he chose to do with his success. He continues to head his church and has even built several new ones in the neighborhood, where they have instituted an incentives program that has worked wonders for the students of the barrio. In exchange for good behavior and proper completion of homework, children in the school can earn fake money as a reward. This money can then be used to purchase necessities in the church store (everything from socks and underwear to street clothes and school uniforms).

177

The beauty of such a program is two-fold. First, in the hopes of gaining something better for themselves (something that is clearly important to the children; something tangible that can be sought after and achieved), the students in an otherwise doomed community have demonstrated vast improvements in their schoolwork. Second, the simple act of working for this fake money offers life training for a large number of children when it comes to the value of real money. If only a few of them learn the joys of honest labor, that is at least a few more young people who won't turn to illegal means in order to make their living.

If only a few children learn the joys of honest labor, that is at least a few more young people who won't turn to illegal means in order to make their living.

There is no reason why such incentives cannot cross cultural boundaries. Many churches of color in America would do well to implement similar incentives programs. Obviously, socks and underwear have far less appeal in the U.S. than they do in the Dominican, but the idea remains the same. Give the children something that they want to work for and they will gladly work. The gift does not have to be a large one, either. For a quarterly grade point average of 2.5, for example, teenage kids in a small, impoverished church could be given a $25 gift certificate to their favorite store. For a 3.5, the child should receive a

$35 gift certificate and so on (the point being that there is a 1 to 1 correlation between dollar value and Grade Point Average). It may not seem like much, but even something as insignificant as $25 has the potential to drive a child a great deal more than a seemingly arbitrary grade. GPA doesn't have to be the only measure of success for a child, either. As truancy and behavior is such an issue in so many public schools, children with high attendance records and exemplary behavior standards can be rewarded similarly to those with an admirable GPA. In addition, for churches that can afford it, a student's GPA or behavioral records can be calculated monthly—perhaps opening up the floor for greater earning potential on the part of the student.

In the absence of any real monetary or proprietary gain, children can be equally rewarded by simply recognizing them in a public setting.

The power of an incentives program is that it removes the "it's all about me" syndrome from the picture. Students are given something outside of themselves to work for, and they often jump at the chance, when it is presented. My son, for example, has a tendency to bug me for the latest video game. Rather than simply buy it for him, I tell him that he has to give me ten green cards from school (at his school, cards are assigned based on behavior standards. A green card is good, while a purple card is bad). I find that every time this kind of incentive is suggested, his behavior continues to excel for weeks; even long after he has reached his goal.

In the absence of any real monetary or proprietary gain, children can be equally rewarded by simply recognizing them in a public setting. What better public setting than in the church itself? It seems rather stunning, the thought of how readily we, as a Black or Brown church institution, criticize those who fail while simultaneously neglecting to recognize those who succeed. Far too many of our best and brightest students go completely unrewarded during their time in the church. As such, there is simply no social separation between a child who is failing out of school and a child who has beaten the odds and gained the accolades necessary to attend college on scholarship.

To combat this all-too-common shortfall in proper recognition, it should be suggested that, if a student achieves a 2.5 or better on his/her quarterly grades, he/she should be celebrated in the church. He/she should be called to stand before his/her peers to be honored. Given this kind of recognition, the average student is more likely to make his/her achievements more the standard than the exception. He/she is liable to continue to get good grades in the future. And, what's more, we will never allow one of our valuable over-achievers to go unrecognized again. This does not have to be relegated to quarterly grades, either. With the detailed reports provided by the Public Education Leader, there is no reason that a child cannot be recognized on a monthly basis. Imagine the benefit on both the psyche and educational outlook of a child if he/she is called to the front of the church on a monthly basis to receive praise regarding his/her academic or behavioral performance.

Another low-cost opportunity to exact real change comes from the idea of an adult in a position of power and authority taking direct responsibility for the actions of a child. Even with an already busy schedule, there is no reason why a pastor or public education leader cannot make it a point to visit the schools of his/her congregation's children and speak directly with the administrators and teachers in charge of said children. Even if the visit is only monthly or quarterly, it speaks to three great needs. The first is that it helps those in the best position to aid our struggling students to come to a greater understanding of where those students stand. The second is that it lets the teachers and administrators who see these same students every day know that there is at least someone who is going to hold them accountable for how they handle their jobs. And the third is that it generates a great deal of shock value in the eyes of most children.

The final point is one to consider deeply. Many (not all, of course, but many) students who fail to meet state-mandated standards simply lack an adult influence to spur them toward improvement. If a child sees his/her church leader out of context, taking an active interest in the activities that fall during the six days that the child isn't in church, the child is likely to respect the reasoning behind the visit. This kind of respect leads to a fear of public repercussions (or at least a good chiding from the minister), which in turn motivates the child to improve. Somebody is watching them, after all.

A Sensible Scholarship Fund

The act of large churches, both minority and White, handing out scholarship funds to adoring young students is not at all uncommon. It should be stated again, however, that the size of these congregations has absolutely nothing to do with their ability to reward their youth. Again, with the sample congregation of 50 adults (and the budget of $6,000 per year), the chances of more than two or three students graduating from high school in a given year are slim.

Say that there are two students graduating from the sample church this year, one who intends to go to junior college and another who plans to attend a four-year university. Now, with the $6,000 budget that this church is working with and the skyrocketing costs of attending college, a full scholarship offer, even to an in-state university, is certainly not in the cards. But a *difference* can still be made.

Say this church has earmarked $1,000 to a yearly scholarship fund. This $1,000 can easily cover the various fees related to application, enrollment and association that often come with entering an institution of higher education. With what is left over, the church can probably even afford to pay for the books that each student will need to begin the semester. These kinds of contributions may not seem like much—but they have the potential to make a world of difference to the average college student.

These kinds of scholarships do not have to come without requirements, either. As alluded to before (and as will be discussed later in the chapter), kids tend to appreciate things more if they have to work for them. Even if a scholarship requires that the student fill out an application, that's something. A compulsory interview process could also be established. Even a work-study program, which could involve mentoring, tutoring, or just checking in on the younger children in the congregation, would not be out of the question.

Obviously, all scholarships should be given on an as-needed basis. Though any church is capable of producing a 4.0 student, academic achievement alone should not be the central motivating factor. Financial need should be the most significant determinant.

> A work-study program, which could involve mentoring, tutoring, or just checking on the younger children in the congregation, would not be out of the question.

The true power of this program, though, is that the $1,000 yearly contribution does not rest in a vacuum. Imagine that, instead of offering the $25 Target gift card for laudable performance, this small church provided a $100 contribution to a specific child's scholarship fund. So, every quarter that one student achieves good grades, that same student earns money for college. Then, during the seven-to ten-year period between the time that the child is able to understand the significance of scholarship funding and when the child is preparing to go away to school, this money can be saved, invested and expanded. That minimum of $400 per year ($100 quarterly) that the student could earn has the potential, then, to make a significant dent in the cost of college. It may not amount to a full scholarship, but at least a portion of each year's tuition could be covered by the church's support—and every little bit counts. In larger congregations, the contribution is magnified, leading to the potential for as much as a full four-year scholarship for the church's best student(s).

> If our children are growing up in our churches, it is our *responsibility* to see to it that they get some assistance for college.

Of course, whenever such numbers are being bandied about (especially when the word "investing" enters the picture) people tend to grow a little wary of contributing. They cannot see exactly what the money is being used for, after all. In response, another report is warranted. This report could potentially be presented by the same pastor-appointed congregant that was discussed earlier. He/she could give a regular presentation on how much money is contained within the scholarship fund, how it's being invested and what it's being used for. When people know what is being done with their money, they are usually a lot less apprehensive about giving. And make no mistake, if our children are growing up in our churches, it is our *responsibility* to see to it that they get some assistance for college. If they have been good enough to attend our churches year after year after year, we should be willing to reward them somehow. Period.

Male Involvement

The key to running a successful outreach program on a shoestring budget is volunteerism. The program that this section outlines is essentially a male mentoring program concept born of the success of the Boys and Girls Club of America and the Big Brother/Sister Association. As mentioned in Chapter 2, the demographic most at risk within the minority community is the teenage male. Many times, this risk can be averted by something as simple as mentorship. Troubled teen males often need little more than a positive male role model to look after their interests.

The extraordinary thing about this condition is that the interests do not even need to be looked after on a daily basis. If the church sponsors one regular program (and it doesn't even have to be a weekly one) that pairs troubled boys (or boys in general) with respectable men who earn honest livings, it stands to make a world of difference. Even if this program is a thirty-minute period during, prior to, or after the church service that requires the men in the congregation to sit and converse with the boys, a great deal of positive change can be made.

Regardless of how far a boy has strayed, the requirement of sharing personal performance with someone they look up to stands the best chance of bringing them back to the path.

The Obvious: Tutoring

The best way to improve the grades of a child who simply has a lesser *capacity* to do well in school is to require the attendance of tutoring programs. These programs stand to help many families fight through the educational problems that often weigh down other aspects of functional living. The only trouble with them is that their cost, for the average family, is nothing short of staggering. Some charge in the neighborhood of $500 per month. Most people, especially people living near the poverty line, can't afford that kind of expense.

With our $6,000 per year, however, these tutorships become more affordable. Also, funding like this has the potential to allow the church to offer its own tutoring programs. Secondhand or refurbished computers can be purchased for a fraction of what they once could. College preparatory courses and practice SATs and ACTs can be obtained at group rates. Math and language development tests and curriculum material is offered to the public for all grade levels and can be purchased to assist struggling students. And of course, the church building itself already offers the perfect setting for extracurricular learning and language training for those who speak English as a second language.

Work Hard/Play Hard

The final point for this chapter is that nobody can achieve a working goal without taking the time to unwind once in a while. Each church group, especially those so centered on improving the educational performance of its members, should take the time and commit the energy to providing social activities that fall outside the realm of scholarship. Such an act not only affords a positive social setting for a child that is constantly exposed to any number of negative ones, it also demonstrates that the adults in his/her life are truly engrossed in what interests him/her. In other words, as parents and church leaders, only if we open our doors to the kids can we expect them to open their doors to us.

It is true that a MegaFest is far beyond the scope of most small churches, but the concepts behind it certainly are not. While at MegaFest they may boast performances by some of the biggest names in hip-hop gospel or Christian comedy, a small church can offer a supervised open mic night for its children to showcase their own talent. Youth forums can be had without significant cost or obligation. Trips to nearby amusement parks, for large groups, are surprisingly affordable. A room in the church can be furnished with games, equipment and other materials that interest kids from ages five to 18. Supervised church lock-ins (or sleepovers) can be remarkably entertaining for both young and old alike.

Housing activities like these for the children tends to get them more involved with the church itself and, therefore, the goals that the church was founded upon. In addition, all social activities can and should be paid for by the money gathered in children-supported fundraisers. If the kids want that Xbox 360 for the church's youth rec. room, tell them that they need to organize a carwash or a bake sale. If they want that trip to Six Flags, they need to cook and serve a fundraising breakfast after a church service or two. Each of these programs keeps children interested in what the church is doing. The more interested they become, the more likely they are to want to improve themselves in the classroom. And the best part about all of it is that it can be paid for on the fundraising and grades-boosting efforts demonstrated by the children themselves.

The Basics

The take-home message for this chapter is that the programs listed above are the *basics*. All of them can be achieved with little (or in some cases no) money at the disposal of the church. With this foundation, the sky is the limit. If enough interest is generated in the children, what the church will be left with is a low-cost and self-sustaining program to boost the educational performance in their own little pocket of the country. Through this comprehensive (but basic) plan, we find the potential to teach the value of money, raise funds for the church and its initiatives and build a large coalition of people working together toward a common goal. This is a take-action kind of approach. It requires the gathering of information and the strengthening of will. Fortunately, those are two things that our people tend to do quite well.

PART FOUR

The Results

Now is the accepted time, not tomorrow, not some more convenient season. It is today that our best work can be done and not some future day or future year. It is today that we fit ourselves for the greater usefulness of tomorrow. Today is the seed time, now are the hours of work, and tomorrow comes the harvest and the playtime.

—*W.E.B. DuBois*

CHAPTER 10

In the Absence of Action:
A Bleak Vision of the Future

If ending on a decidedly bleak note may be allowed, it does not seem unreasonable to suggest that, in the event that these startling educational numbers do not take at least a moderate turn for the better, before us stretches an unwelcome projection of the future for an unhealthy portion of the next generation of children of color. The true horror of this scenario is that, as a minority people, we are not faced with simply a few school years of shortfalls. This future will have been decades in the making. Owed to many long years of educational underperformance, small pockets of every city and town in America will likely be afflicted by the plague of ignorance and apathy that the current culture seems so tacitly disposed to promote.

This book does not suggest that we cannot right the wrongs of the recent past. There is still a window of opportunity shining all-inviting and sunlit before us. Since it is not yet too late (assuming that the church becomes willing to finally take a stand), what we, as parents and church leaders, need to uncover is the tipping point. We need to dig beneath the numbers to reveal the specific signs that signal a culture that has spiraled out of control. So, in the hopes of shedding some light on the subject, let us take the time to reexamine the trends that fuel such a fatalistic viewpoint.

Declining Scores

To begin a quick reiteration of the hard figures presented in Chapter 2, urban schools demonstrate an average of a 40% graduation rate among minority students. Across the board, 56% of young Black females complete four years of high school while only 43% of young Black males live up to the task. Hispanic students do not fare much better. For them, the dropout rate is 44.2%. In every state-mandated testing category, Blacks and Hispanics scored far lower than White and Asian students. The average GPA for minority girls is 2.2 while the average for minority boys is 1.85. An inordinately small number of Black and Brown students register for Advanced Placement classes as well, clocking in at nearly a 10% lower rate than White students in almost every category.

While many of their White counterparts are seeking advanced jobs via the route of four-year degrees, many college-age Black students seem to view a two-year degree as the answer (nearly 70% of all junior college enrollees are Black). Of the abnormally small number of Black men and women who enter a four-year school, only 40% reach graduation. In 2000, Hispanics accounted for 11% of high school graduates in America. Only 7% of those graduates went on to attend a four-year university.

The trouble with the numbers presented above is that, in order to get into a position of power in this country, one must obtain a presentable level of education. One cannot find a teaching job and is very unlikely to grab a political seat without holding a college degree. So, to those who claim that this bleak viewpoint is too narrow—that the real answer lies in more African-American and Hispanic people taking strides to gain political office and other positions of power—the following question should be asked: How are these people supposed to lead if they do not have the credentials to do so?

Certainly, it is true that there still remains great numbers of Black and Brown people in America that are willing and able to effectively lead the masses towards a brighter future. To ignore the Barack Obamas or the Mel Martinezes of the world would obviously be folly. The problem is not in the *ability* to develop the kinds of minds it takes to shift the thinking of an entire populace (as a proud and fiercely loyal set of racial subgroups, we are still quite capable of raising the next Martin Luther King Jr., after all); the problem is the *propensity* or even the *probability* that we can do so. In a minority nation that needs dozens and perhaps hundreds of capable leaders in order to see any real change through to the end, it certainly does not help to lose almost half of our young people to the jaws of greed, ignorance and apathy. Is it not fair to think that the more children we lose, the greater our chances become of losing a would-be leader? Is it not fair to believe that the farther our children fall, the more our hope is darkened?

With *Beyond Role Models: An Examination of Cultural Influences on the Pedagogical Perspectives of Black Teachers*, author Jacqueline Jordan Irvine states that "the increasing alienation and school failure of minorities, particularly the growing numbers of at-risk Black students, is directly related to the decline of minority teachers who bring to the classroom unique, culturally based pedagogical approaches that are often compatible with the learning needs of their minority students." Taking things a step further, it can be stated that, with a youth culture that increasingly distrusts the establishment, the most logical solution to overcome such ignorance is to build an environment full of positive Black and Brown role models. Unfortunately, as the above article shows, there are fewer and fewer such people in the educational world each year. "By the year 2020, 39% of the school-age population will be minority; yet data predict that the minority teaching force will be 5%." Essentially, we cannot expect the number of qualified teachers to improve either, as long as our students continue to avoid AP classes, fail to graduate from high school and reject the idea of the four-year college.

The state of U.S. politics, too, seems rather austere for the minority citizen. With a ruling body that boasts only five minority Senators (only one of which is Black), 62 minority members of congress (out of 435 seats) and four minority members of the White House Cabinet, the future looks far less promising. In the absence of vast fortunes or familial power, the traditional path to Washington runs through law school. Today, according to American Bar Association statistics, law school enrollment among African Americans has decreased by 2% since 2000 (while there has been a simultaneous increase of overall law school enrollment of 20%). In a nation with a total of only 71 Black and Brown political leaders in Washington, a shrinking pool of potential candidates is not likely to improve matters. And the trouble with this kind of backslide is that it can only lead to greater peril for our offspring.

A Generation at Risk

Imagine a generation with a mass contingent of maladjusted children that fail to surpass their parents in education. Take the time to ponder that concept. From the time of slavery or first immigration, people of color have managed to better themselves with almost every passing decade. The parent who could not read managed to raise children who at least finished a significant portion of primary school. This modestly educated child grew up to parent children who proudly graduated from high school and began working independent and decently paying jobs. This intrepid worker bred a new group of children ready to head to college and the brightest future that our people have ever seen.

Somewhere along the line, however, that final step was interrupted—held down as though weighted at the neck. And history has seen a hiccup in the plan which threatens to turn the entire progression on its head, sending it reeling back to the exact kind of dependency that our forebears were so intrepidly trying to avoid.

As the rate of education dips, the rate of welfare need soars in the most impoverished and entrapped regions of the country. The more people depend on the state, the more the state falls short of its funding needs for schools in those same impoverished areas, as well. With Black and Brown people as a whole

With Black and Brown people as a whole continuing to work below the poverty line and collect welfare at an almost 25% rate, it is difficult to imagine poor performance in school adding anything positive to the outlook.

continuing to work below the poverty line and collect welfare at an almost 25% rate, it is difficult to imagine poor performance in school adding anything positive to the outlook.

At the same time, Black and Brown society will enter what is arguably the third generation of babies having babies. While, according to www.teenpregnancy.org, the numbers regarding minority teen pregnancy (particularly among young Black women) have shown a rather encouraging trend since the early 90s, the informational website goes on to reveal that the future tends to be directly linked to school performance. In addition, "the children of teenage mothers…are more likely to perform poorly in school…are 13% more likely to end up in prison…[and] are 22% more likely to become teen mothers themselves." Each young woman who follows this path endangers her own children to a life of relative independence. The more independent a child is forced to be, the more likely he/she is to stray from the path of true advancement.

For every failure, in other words, there are at least three success stories. But the problem is that we still have that 25% to worry about.

Lack of healthcare, the expansion of poverty, increased political entrapment, a steady and unacceptable rate of unemployment and an embarrassing contingent of illiterate adults; all will be magnified in the coming years. The more we succumb to the pain of paying for medical attention, the more we fail to make ends meet, the more we continue to vote for politicians who do not truly have our interests at heart, the more we collect welfare, the more the source of the problem perpetuates itself.

The Prevailing Hope

As mentioned in Chapters 8 and 9, there is still a great deal of hope in which to put stock. Outreach programs *are* effective within the small circles that they directly affect. The problem is not that we lack a desire to help; the problem is that the web we have cast is far too small or sporadic. Unless the kinds of programs highlighted in Chapter 9 or demonstrated by the Great Eight, the St. Jude Baptist Church, the NAACP, Mount Zion Baptist Church and the Urban League are instituted and well-planned in every community in America, we will continue to see a mere middling effort. Advancement will continue in some categories and regress in others.

Nearly 75% of the people in the Black and Brown communities in this country lead comfortable, educated and productive lives. For every failure, in other words, there are at least three success stories. But the problem is that we still have that 25% to worry about. And given the trends demonstrated by this particular group of Americans, an expansion of their membership is far more likely than a decline.

Fighting the Quicksand

Where do things for our people begin to go terribly awry, beyond possibility of recognition or repair? The trouble with this question is that it is almost impossible to predict. One measure that can be assumed, however, is that declining educational numbers spell doom for a large population of people in the very near future. This statement can be made simply because education represents the center of all things in America. This is a country built on a sweeping and noble enterprising tradition. It remains a country where anyone can get ahead, so long as they are willing to take what they want (and are willing to work to gain the power to do so). Make no mistake, in American society, the single greatest way to take action and get ahead is to complete the studies related to the educational constructs that this country was founded upon.

If we may think of prosperity as a kind of long-distance run, then those who succeed are clearly the ones who run the fastest or most strategic race. As with anything of this nature, getting ahead takes discipline and a good deal of training. Unfortunately, without at least a moderate education, our children are destined to lack the training and discipline they need. They are destined to be behind the pack before the race even begins. And as the figures show, a decline in educational numbers tends to lead to a whole host of other cultural problems that make it very difficult to reverse the trend.

If school performance continues to deteriorate, then the negative issues facing a large contingent of people of color begin to mushroom. It is not unreasonable to predict that continued failure in the school system will lead to more dropouts (as the numbers have and will certainly continue to show). The more dropouts, the more drug dealers. The more drug dealers, the more dependency issues. The more dependency issues, the more welfare. The more welfare, the more teen pregnancy. The more teen pregnancy, the more children are raised by parents who are, quite frankly, babies themselves. And the cycle repeats itself, eventually becoming self-perpetuating.

As Black and Brown people in America, we have been raised on a long and proud tradition of steadfast determination. In the face of the greatest adversity, we have a remarkable history and beautiful capacity to rise above the turmoil and hate, to etch out a higher path for ourselves. From Frederick Douglass to Dr. King, we as a people have managed to get by in a world that would seek to tread upon us. But somewhere along the line, we lost our way. Somewhere along the line, we forgot that age-old wisdom that children are our greatest asset.

Throughout the past two centuries, our people have bared witness to travail and triumph. We have come so far as a nation, but it seems as though there are still many aspects of our lives that have slipped back to the brink of disaster. It is as if we have climbed from the deepest pit to the very crest of the American social mountain and, just before reaching the summit, we have lost our footing. Now, it is as though we have found ourselves waist-deep in a pool of deadly quicksand. As is the case with quicksand, we must remain calm and thoughtful if we hope to dig our way out. Oftentimes, when facing near-death, it may seem like the first and most logical course of action would be to seek help from someone with the power to offer aid; someone standing beside us on dry ground. Support, though, will not be handed to us. The life preserver will not come from Capitol Hill. And if the parents of troubled children are either unwilling or unable to kick against the falling current, then in the end, only the church of color, with its powerful voice and its tremendous cultural potential, holds the line to pull us all back to safety. The question then remains: will it heed our cry for help?